Also by Mark Baimbridge

From Rome to Maastricht: A Reappraisal of Britain's Membership of the European Community (*co-author*)

There is an Alternative: Britain and its Relationship with the EU (*co-author*)

The Impact of the Euro: Debating Britain's Future (*co-editor*)

Economic and Monetary Union in Europe: Theory, Evidence and Practice (*co-editor*)

Fiscal Federalism and European Economic Integration (*co-editor*)

Current Economic Issues in EU Integration (*co-author*)

Britain and the European Union: Alternative Futures (*co-author*)

Implications of the Euro: A Critical Perspective from the Left (*co-editor*)

The 1975 Referendum on Europe: Current Analysis and Lessons for the Future (*co-author*)

The 1975 Referendum on Europe: Reflections of the Participants (*editor*)

Britain, the Euro and Beyond (*co-author*)

Britain in a Global World: Options for a New Beginning (*editor*)

Also by Philip B. Whyman

There is an Alternative: Britain and its Relationship with the EU (*co-author*)

The Impact of the Euro: Debating Britain's Future (*co-editor*)

Economic and Monetary Union in Europe: Theory, Evidence and Practice (*co-editor*)

Fiscal Federalism and European Economic Integration (*co-editor*)

Sweden and the 'Third Way': A Macroeconomic Evaluation

An Analysis of the Economic Democracy Reforms in Sweden

Britain and the European Union: Alternative Futures (*co-author*)

Implications of the Euro: A Critical Perspective from the Left *(co-editor)*

'Third Way' Economics: An Evaluation *(author)*

The 1975 Referendum on Europe: Current Analysis and Lessons for the Future (*co-author*)

Britain, the Euro and Beyond (*co-author*)

Britain in a Global World: Options for a New Beginning *(editor)*

Also by Brian Burkitt

Trade Unions and Wages: Implications for Economic Theory *(author)*

Trade Unions and the Economy (*co-author*)

Radical Political Economy *(author)*

The Political Economy of Social Credit and Guild Socialism (*co-author*)

The Impact of the Euro: Debating Britain's Future (*co-editor*)

Britain and the European Union: Alternative Futures (*co-author*)

Implications of the Euro: A Critical Perspective from the Left *(co-editor)*

Britain in a Global World: Options for a New Beginning *(editor)*

Moored to the Continent?
Future Options for Britain and the EU

Mark Baimbridge
Division of Economics
School of Social and International Studies
University of Bradford, UK

Philip B. Whyman
Lancashire Institute for Economic and Business Research
Lancashire Business School
University of Central Lancashire, UK

Brian Burkitt
Department of Social Sciences and Humanities,
School of Social and International Studies,
University of Bradford, UK

TABLE OF CONTENTS

PREFACE

There are many people to thank for their input into making this book possible. We would like to thank our colleagues at the universities of Bradford and Central Lancashire for their comradeship and general support for our research on European economic integration. Finally, we owe a deep sense of gratitude to our families and partners for their forbearance during the preparation of this book. It is to them that this book is dedicated: MB: Mary, Ken, Beibei and Douglas; PW: Barbara, Boyd and Claire; BB: Beryl, Ivan and Marvin.

Any remaining errors and omissions we gladly attribute to each other.

Haworth, Nether Edge and Guiseley
April 2011

EUROPEAN INTEGRATION TIMELINE

From its beginnings, half a century ago, in the immediate aftermath of World War II, through to its expansion, we highlight some of the key events that have shaped the development of the EU towards closer integration.

1948	The **Organisation for European Economic Cooperation (OEEC)** is set up in Paris in April 1948, coordinating the distribution of the Marshall Plan financial aid that will amount to $12.5 billion from 1948 to 1951. The OEEC consists of one representative from each of the 17 Western European countries that join the organisation. In May 1948 in The Hague, the Congress of Europe (a meeting of delegates from 16 European countries) agree to form the **Council of Europe** with the aim of establishing closer economic and social ties.
1951	The **European Coal and Steel Community (ECSC)** is established by the signing of the Treaty of Paris in April 1951. Along with France and West Germany, Italy, Belgium, Luxembourg and The Netherlands have also chosen to join the organisation. Members of the ECSC pledge to remove all import duties and quota restrictions on the trade of coal, iron ore, and steel between the member states.
1952	The **European Defence Community (EDC)** Treaty is signed by France, West Germany, Italy, Belgium, Holland and Luxembourg in May 1952. It includes provision for the formation of a parallel **European Political Community (EPC)**. However both initiatives are destined to founder since the French National Assembly never ratifies the EDC Treaty, finally rejecting it in August 1954.
1955	The process of further European integration is given fresh

	impetus by a conference of ECSC foreign ministers at Messina, Italy, in June 1955. The meeting agrees to develop the community by encouraging free trade between member states through the removal of tariffs and quotas. Agreement is also reached to form an Atomic Energy Community to encourage co-operation in the nuclear energy industry.
1958	The two Treaties of Rome are signed, establishing the **European Economic Community (EEC)** and the **European Atomic Energy Community (Euratom)**. As well as stipulating the eventual removal of customs duties on trade between member countries (over a period of 12 years) the EEC Treaty sets out to allow the free movement of workers, capital and services across borders and to harmonise policies on agriculture and transport
1960	At the Stockholm Convention in January 1960, Austria, Britain, Denmark, Norway, Portugal, Sweden and Switzerland form the **European Free Trade Association (EFTA)**. The objective of EFTA is to promote free trade but without the formal structures of the EEC.
1961	UK applies to join the EEC.
1963	British application for EEC membership fails.
1967	UK submits second application to join EEC.
1968	Customs union completed and **Common Agricultural Policy** enacted.
1972	In October, following the recommendations of the **Werner Report**, the EEC launches its first attempt at harmonising exchange rates. The mechanism adopted is the so called 'snake in the tunnel' whereby participating governments are required to confine the fluctuations of their currencies within a range of +/- 1% against each other. The value of the group of currencies (the snake) is also to be maintained within a range of +/-2.25% against the US dollar (the tunnel). Countries requiring assistance to keep their currencies within the required band may receive help only in the form of loans
1973	Denmark, Ireland and the UK join the EEC.
1975	UK referendum supports staying in EEC.
1978	At a summit in Bremen in July, the French and West

	German governments announce their intention to create the **European Monetary System (EMS)**. At the centre of the EMS is the **European Currency Unit (ECU)**. The value of the ECU is to be derived from a weighted basket of all participating currencies with the greatest weighting against the West German mark.
1981	Greece joins the EC.
1986	Portugal and Spain join the EC.
1990	UK joins EMS.
1992	At a summit of the European Council in Maastricht, Holland, the **Treaty on European Union (TEU)**, also known as the Maastricht Treaty, is signed. Originally intended to include a declaration of an intention to move towards federal union, at Britain's insistence this aspect is played down. Subsequent to the signing of the Maastricht Treaty, the European Community is referred to as the **European Union (EU)**. UK leaves EMS.
1993	The Single European Market takes effect. Trade tariffs are scrapped, but Duty Free shopping remains until 1999.
1994	Stage 2 of EMU is initiated on 1 January with the establishment of the **European Monetary Institute (EMI)** to oversee the co-ordination of the monetary policies of the individual national central banks. The EMI will also work towards the introduction of Stage 3 by organising the creation of the European Central Bank.
1995	Austria, Finland and Sweden join the EU, bringing membership to 15. The **Schengen agreement** comes into force and scraps border controls. UK and Ireland stay out of the agreement.
1997	Heads of government draft a new agreement in Amsterdam that updates the Maastricht Treaty and prepares the EU for its eastward expansion. Qualified majority voting is introduced into new areas, reducing individual countries' powers to veto new measures.
1998	At the beginning of May, at a summit of EU officials and heads of state in Brussels, the announcement is made as to which countries will participate in the launch of the euro

	the following January. In June the **European Central Bank (ECB)** is established in Frankfurt, Germany. The ECB together with the national central banks of the 15 EU member states form the **European System of Central Banks (ESCB)** which will be responsible for setting monetary policy for the euro countries and managing those countries' foreign reserves. The EU opens accession negotiations with Hungary, Poland, Estonia, the Czech Republic, Slovenia and Cyprus.
1999	Romania, Slovakia, Latvia, Lithuania, Bulgaria and Malta are invited to begin accession negotiations. Eleven countries adopt the euro as their official currency (although national currency notes and coins remain in circulation), but Sweden, Denmark and the UK stay out.
2000	The Nice summit agrees to limit the size of the Commission and increase the president's powers. Qualified majority voting is introduced in new areas, but members keep their vetoes on social security and tax. A timetable for taking forward accession negotiations is endorsed.
2001	The Laeken European Council establishes the **Convention on the Future of Europe**.
2002	Euro notes and coins are introduced in 12 EU countries. The European Commission announces that 10 countries are on course to meet the criteria for accession to the EU in 2004.
2003	The UK has been a member of the EU for 30 years.
2004	EU enlargement to 25 member states with addition of Slovakia, Latvia, Lithuania, Malta, Hungary, Poland, Estonia, the Czech Republic, Slovenia and Cyprus.
2005	**EU Constitution** ratification ended by referendum defeats in France and the Netherlands. The UK holds EU Presidency, but fails to make progress on new 2007–13 budget. Accession negotiations are opened with Turkey and Croatia.

2006	Slovenia's entry into the euro on 1 January 2007 is confirmed. Accession negotiations with Turkey are suspended.
2007	EU enlargement to 27 member states with addition of Bulgaria and Romania.
2008	Slovenia becomes the first of the recent enlargement members to hold the Presidency of the Council of the EU. **Treaty of Lisbon** ratification ended by referendum defeat in Ireland.
2009	Final year of the **Barroso Commission**. Seventh series of elections to the **European Parliament**. Second referendum on the **Treaty of Lisbon** in Ireland.
2010	Spain is the first country to hold the presidency under the Lisbon Treaty and the new '**trio presidency system**' working with Belgium and Hungary. Heads of state and government agree to support the Greek government in its efforts to meet the Stability Programme targets for 2010. European Council adopts a 10-year strategy for smart, sustainable and inclusive growth: Europe 2020. The EU agrees to support the **Irish** economy to help safeguard the stability of the euro.
2011	**Estonia** adopts the euro, becoming the seventeenth member of the euro area. The first '**European semester**' of economic policy coordination between EU countries to help prevent economic crises like the one in 2008–10. A comprehensive package of measures to strengthen the European economy is finalised with the **Euro Plus Pact** to reinforce economic policy coordination in the EMU.

GLOSSARY OF TERMS

Asymmetric and symmetric external shocks	External shocks refer to the impact upon the domestic economy generated by activities beyond the control of UK authorities, for example a sudden rise in oil prices or change in global demand for raw materials. If an external shock has a similar effect amongst a given group of countries, it is said to be a *symmetric* shock since the policy response will be largely the same for all countries. *Asymmetric* shocks, alternatively, refer to those changes in the external environment that have significantly different effects upon different countries, requiring very different policy responses by each country in order to respond effectively.
Common Agricultural Policy (CAP)	EU agricultural support scheme which accounts for majority of EU budget until 1997. The protection of EU food producers has led to food prices rising significantly higher than world prices.
Commonwealth	The Commonwealth of Nations, usually known as The Commonwealth, is an association of independent sovereign states, almost all of which are former territories of the British Empire. The Commonwealth is primarily an organisation in which countries with diverse economic backgrounds have an opportunity for close and equal interaction. The primary activities of the Commonwealth are designed to create an atmosphere of economic cooperation between member nations, as well as the promotion of democracy, human rights, and good governance in them. The Commonwealth is not a political union of any sort, and does not allow the UK to exercise any power over the affairs of the organisation's other members. The Commonwealth encompasses a population of approximately 1.8 billion people, making up about 30% of the world's total, whilst the land area of the Commonwealth nations equals about a 25% of the world's land area.
Cyclical and structural convergence	Economic convergence refers to potential EMU participants becoming economically similar prior to membership. Cyclical convergence occurs when the business cycles of boom and recession become

	increasingly similar amongst participating economies, so that a recession in the UK would occur approximately at the same time as a comparable slow-down in Germany, rather than one or two years in advance as at present. Similarly, structural convergence refers to changes in industrial and financial structure of the participating economies that have the effect of ensuring similar reactions to external forces over the long term.
Deflation/ reflation	Deflation may be defined as a reduction in economic activity in the economy that is associated with a sustained reduction in inflation, output and employment. Reflation refers to an increase in economic activity that stimulates output, employment and inflation in varying degrees.
Devaluation/ revaluation/ over-valuation	Devaluation refers to a reduction in the value of a given exchange rate relative to other rates, whilst revaluation concerns the increase in the exchange rate. For example, if the exchange rate on a given day was £1 equals $1.67, if the value of sterling increased so that £1 could now buy $2 worth of goods, the value of the pound would be said to have appreciated, whereas if the value fell to perhaps $1.5, sterling would be said to have fallen in value or devalued. Over-valuation refers to the circumstance where the value of sterling is so high that British exporters find it difficult to compete and possibly lead to a trade deficit where more is imported than exported. Too high an over-valuation could lead to economic recession as export companies reduce output and lay off workers. This then may spread to the remainder of the economy.
Economic and Monetary Union (EMU)	As a matter of definition, monetary union occurs when exchange rates are *permanently and irrevocably* fixed and may therefore precede the introduction of a single currency. However, the two terms are generally used interchangeably. Economic union involves a further transfer of macroeconomic policy to the federal level—particularly monetary policy but typically also 'coordination' of fiscal policy within prescribed limits.
European Central Bank (ECB)	This supersedes national central banks in those EU nations participating in EMU. Based in Frankfurt, the ECB will be in sole charge of exchange rate and monetary policy for all EMU countries, setting one common interest rate which will apply irrespective of the particular needs of individual countries at any period of

	time. Its sole policy goal is to achieve price stability without a similar responsibility to assist employment creation or economic growth. Policy conflict between ECB and the wider economic responsibilities of individual governments is difficult to resolve since the ECB is beyond the control of both member states and the EU Commission.
European Economic Area (EEA)	The European Economic Area (EEA) came into being on 1 January 1994 following an agreement between the European Free Trade Association (EFTA) and the EU. It was designed to allow EFTA countries to participate in the European SIM without having to join the EU. In an obligatory referendum, Switzerland's citizens chose not to participate in the EEA. Instead, the Swiss are linked to the EU by bilateral agreements, with a different content than that of the EEA agreement. Thus, the current members, contracting parties, are three of the four EFTA states (Iceland, Liechtenstein and Norway) and the EU25. The EEA is based on 4 'freedoms': the free movement of goods, persons, services and capital between the EEA countries. The non-EU members of the EEA have agreed to enact legislation similar to that passed in the EU in the areas of Social Policy, Consumer Protection, Environment, Company Law and Statistics.
European Financial Stability Facility (EFSF)	The European Financial Stability Facility (EFSF) is a special purpose vehicle agreed by the EU27 on 9 May 2010, aiming at preserving financial stability in the eurozone by providing financial assistance to eurozone states in economic difficulty. The European Investment Bank provides treasury management services and administrative support. The EFSF can issue bonds or other debt instruments on the market with the support of the German Debt Management Office to raise the funds needed to provide loans to eurozone countries in financial difficulties recapitalise banks or buy sovereign debt. Bonds would be backed by guarantees given by the euro area member states in proportion to their share in the paid-up capital of the European Central Bank (ECB). The Facility may be combined with loans up to €60 billion from the EFSM and up to €250 billion from the International Monetary Fund (IMF) to obtain a financial safety net up to €750 billion. The EFSF can only act after a support request is made by a eurozone member and when a country programme has been negotiated with the European Commission and the IMF, together with its unanimous acceptance by the eurogroup.

European Financial Stabilisation Mechanism (EFSM)	The European Financial Stabilisation Mechanism (EFSM) is an emergency funding programme reliant upon funds raised on the financial markets and guaranteed by the European Commission using the EU budget as collateral. It runs under the supervision of the Commission and aims at preserving financial stability by providing financial assistance to EU member states in economic difficulty. The Commission fund, backed by all 27 member states, has the authority to raise up to €60 billion.
European Free Trade Association (EFTA)	The European Free Trade Association (EFTA) was established on 3 May 1960 as an alternative for European states that were not allowed or did not wish to join the EU. The treaty was signed on 4 January 1960 in Stockholm by seven states (United Kingdom, Denmark, Norway, Sweden, Austria, Switzerland and Portugal). Finland became an associate member in 1961 (later becoming a full member in 1986), whilst Iceland joined in 1970. The United Kingdom, Denmark and Ireland joined the EU in 1973, and hence ceased to be EFTA members, whilst Portugal left EFTA for the EU in 1986. Liechtenstein joined in 1991 (previously its interests in EFTA had been represented by Switzerland). Finally, Austria, Sweden and Finland joined the EU in 1995 and hence ceased to be EFTA members. Currently, only Iceland, Norway, Switzerland and Liechtenstein remain members of EFTA. The EFTA States have jointly concluded free trade agreements with a number of countries worldwide. EFTA has the following institutions: the Secretariat, the EFTA Council, the EFTA Surveillance Authority, and the EFTA Court.
European Stability Mechanism (ESM)	The European Stability Mechanism (ESM) is a permanent rescue funding programme to succeed the temporary EFSF and EFSM, due to be launched in mid-2013 with the European Commission, rather than EU member states, playing a central role in its operation. On 16 December 2010, the European Council agreed an amendment to the Lisbon Treaty that would avoid any referendums, which read 'The member states whose currency is the euro may establish a stability mechanism to be activated if indispensable to safeguard the stability of the euro area as a whole. The granting of any required financial assistance under the mechanism will be made subject to strict conditionality.'
Fiscal policy	Fiscal policy refers to the interaction between

	government expenditure and taxation. Under EMU, fiscal policy will remain under the control of national economic authorities, although constrained by the MCC and *Stability and Growth Pact* rules.
Gross Domestic Product (GDP)/ Gross National Product (GNP)	These are two methods of measuring the value of the total flow of goods and services produced by an economy over a specified period of time—usually a year. The difference between the two is that GNP equals GDP *plus* net income earned by domestic residents from overseas investments.
Maastricht Convergence Criteria	Established by the Maastricht Treaty to ensure economic convergence amongst potential participants prior to their entry to EMU, there are five criteria which each country must achieve before they are permitted to participate in the single currency. They are: (i) each country's rate of inflation must be no more than 1.5% above the average of the lowest three inflation rates in the EMS; (ii) its long-term interest rates must be within 2% of the same three countries chosen for the previous condition; (iii) it must have been a member of the narrow band of fluctuation of the ERM for at least two years without a realignment; (iv) its budget deficit must not be regarded as 'excessive' by the European Council, with 'excessive' defined to be where deficits are greater than 3% of GDP for reasons other than those of a 'temporary' or 'exceptional' nature; (v) its national debt must not be 'excessive', defined as where it is above 60% of GDP and is not declining at a 'satisfactory' pace.
Monetary policy	Monetary policy is typically concerned with the level of interest rates, the availability of credit, banking regulations and the control of the money supply by the central bank. Under EMU, monetary policy will be transferred from national authorities to the ECB.
Nominal and real wage rigidity	Nominal wages refer to money wages, whereas real wages refer to the purchasing power of those wages. Thus, a 3% rise in nominal wages during a period of 2% inflation produces a 1% rise in real wages. Wage rigidity refers to a situation that occurs when wages are observed not to be perfectly flexible in response to a change in economic circumstances, for example, if wages should fail to fall sufficiently to price people back into work during a recession.
North American	The North American Free Trade Agreement (NAFTA)

Free Trade Agreement (NAFTA)	came into effect on 1 January 1994 and links Canada, the United States, and Mexico in a free trade sphere. NAFTA called for immediately eliminating duties on half of all US goods shipped to Mexico and gradually phasing out other tariffs over a period of about 14 years. Restrictions were to be removed from many categories, including motor vehicles and automotive parts, computers, textiles, and agriculture. The treaty also protected intellectual property rights (patents, copyrights, and trademarks) and outlined the removal of restrictions on investment amongst the three countries. Provisions regarding worker and environmental protection were added later as an expansion of the earlier Canada–US Free Trade Agreement of 1989. Unlike the EU, it does not create a set of supranational governmental bodies, nor does it create a body of law that is superior to national law. NAFTA, as an international agreement, is very similar to a treaty. The agreement was initially pursued by free-trade governments in the US and Canada. Some opposition persists to the present day, although labour unions in Canada have recently removed objections to the agreement from their platforms.
Optimum currency area (OCA) theory	This theory is utilised by economists to identify those factors that indicate the *optimum* size of a currency arrangement. Consequently, the theory proposes that objective tests can be employed to decide whether it is in the common interests of, for example, Ireland and Italy, or France and Germany, whether they should join together in EMU, or whether it is in their mutual advantage to retain separate currencies and monetary systems. Similarly, the theory could be used to identify whether *regions*, rather than countries, should form a currency union. Thus, the South-east of England may have more in common with certain wealthy regions of Germany and France than either Wales or Northern Ireland, and in theory it may make economic sense to form a currency arrangement accordingly. In practice, however, whilst nation states remain the principal form of government for the majority of the world's population, OCA theory will be concerned in deciding where monetary integration should and should not be formed between groups of countries.
Single European Act (SEA)	The 1986 Single European Act introduced the single internal market, but also extended qualified majority voting within the Council of Ministers and further committed the EU to 'the objective of the progressive

	realisation of European and Monetary Union'.
Single European Market (SEM)/ Single Internal Market (SIM)	Resulting from the 1986 Single European Act, the single market refers to the removal of trade, capital and physical barriers across Europe, supposedly achieved by 1 January 1993, which allows the free competition across the entire EU market.
Stability and Growth Pact (SGP)	Proposed by Germany to avoid excessive fiscal profligacy by individual member states within EMU, it limits budget deficits to 3% of GDP (as per MCC prior to membership). If this limit is ignored, and the country is not in recession (defined as GDP falling by 0.75%), fines of between 0.2 and 0.5% of GDP will be levied by the EU financial authorities. The Stability and Growth Pact additionally suggests that budget deficits be limited to 1% of GDP in the long term, thus increasing fiscal tightening.

CHAPTER 1

MOORED TO THE CONTINENT?

Since Britain applied for membership of the Common Market in 1961, the issue of the precise nature of the relationship between the UK and the EU has been central to economic and political debate. The momentum behind Britain's application grew rapidly after the Suez crisis in 1956. It possessed two origins, politically it was felt that Britain had lost its worldwide role with the dissolution of Empire and that the future belonged to regional blocs rather than the nation state; economically, it was observed that during the 1950s and 1960s British living standards grew less rapidly than those of most advanced industrial nations, particularly compared to the countries on the continent of Europe that signed the Treaty of Rome committing them to 'ever closer union' in 1957. Therefore, to most members of the British establishment, it seemed obvious that joining the process towards greater European integration would reverse the county's declining political influence and accelerate its rate of economic growth.

A recurrent theme in the British argument is that UK participation in ever closer European economic, and then political, integration is widely perceived as 'inevitable', because withdrawal from the process would leave Britain isolated and largely powerless, both inside and outside the continent to which it belongs. To cite a familiar phrase, 'there is no alternative'. However, we argue in this book that these contentions are spurious. Britain does possess an effective choice between an essentially European future and a comprehensive global strategy; thus the investigation of these possibilities, in the light of some 40 years of EU membership, is the major feature of this book.

The relationship between the UK and the European Union (EU) is one of the defining issues of our times. It is the issue, more than any other, which polarises opinion, dividing members of all of the major political parties, trade unions and business organisations. Supporters of a closer relationship speak of the UK moving to the 'heart of Europe', whereas sceptics and opponents debate variants related to the loosening or fracturing of present arrangements, thereby seeking a greater degree of independence. For advocates of broader and deeper European integration, the 'project' enables each member state to deal more effectively with the pressures arising from globalisation, as a larger economic entity is less likely to be blown off course by the winds of economic turbulence. Similarly, the pooling of sovereignty is presented as a means of retaining effective, collective decision-making for the European region, and thereby enhancing democratic control over events. For opponents and sceptics, the European project has resulted in less transparent, democratically accountable policy determination, with regulations and economic structures that impinge upon democratically determined priorities and preferred national self-management.

In this volume, *Moored to the Continent?*, we explore these themes. In the first section, the awkward partnership between the UK and the EU is appraised. Chapter 2 examines the myth of globalisation and economic interdependence, whereby one of the most influential arguments in favour of continued European integration relates to the assertion that an increased internationalisation, or globalisation, of the world economy has created a new environment which has eroded the efficiency of traditional policy instruments and with it the relevance of individual nation states. Additionally, the shift towards liberalisation of markets amongst most major economies, has given rise to a hyper-globalisation thesis, which claims that the integration of financial markets, the free movement of capital and the rising importance of Trans-National Corporations (TNCs) in global manufacturing production has undermined the abilities of nation states to successfully manage their own affairs. Consequently, European integration is presented as a potential solution to the dilution of national autonomy resulting from these changes. However, there is an inherent contradiction within this standpoint as regional integration represents both a response towards, and expression of, globalisation whereby advocates differ wildly as to the reasons for this conclusion. Chapter 2, therefore, offers an overview of these arguments and insights as to how the hyper-globalisation thesis is largely incorrect in its more far-reaching conclusions.

Subsequently, Chapter 3 discusses the notion of Britain and the EU being geographically so close yet frequently far apart through providing an overview of the historical relationship between the UK and the EU. It summarises why the EU is a distinctive entity compared to the other international organisations to which Britain is aligned; it is from this perspective of the unique interrelationship between Britain and the EU that many, if not all, of the tensions emanate. The turbulent 'on-off' relationship that characterised the post World War II period, the most recent examples of which can be traced back to the 1988 Bruges speech of Mrs Thatcher, has developed to the point where UK membership is being openly questioned. Finally, this chapter addresses potential causes (e.g. the UK's unbroken history, the legacy of empire and war, the presence of a distinctive legal system, unique capitalist structure and an individualistic culture) for the often-fractious relationship between Britain and its continental neighbours.

Part I of the book is concluded by Chapter 4 that examines the consequences of EU membership whereby the UK's relationship with the EU has been controversial, whilst public opinion polls since the early 1990s demonstrate a majority opinion amongst the UK electorate that remains critical of the EU, with a not insignificant number desiring withdrawal. In the face of such apparent hostility towards further economic and political integration, the British establishment has remained remarkably united not only in supporting continued membership of the EU, but in fostering wider and deeper economic integration. Furthermore, the claim is repeatedly made that even a slight weakening in the trend towards greater unification would cost the UK jobs and influence, never mind what would occur if the UK voted to withdraw from EU membership. Yet, governments have been remarkably reticent to undertake an independent cost-benefit analysis of UK membership. Therefore, this chapter reviews the negative trade effects arising from more protectionist policies being imposed upon a nation built upon the principles of free trade, the costs arising from the operation of the Common Agricultural Policy and Common Fisheries Policy, net budget contributions and imposition of EU regulations upon the domestic economy. Certain of these regulations were undoubtedly positive, such as pressures to improve the cleanliness of beaches and certain health and safety rules, whereas others were less welcome and occasionally rather bizarre, such as the insistence upon metric measurement and initiatives relating to pedantic levels of harmonisation.

The second section of the book seeks to broaden the scope of literature in this field of European integration through considering a series of potential alternative relationships between the UK and the EU to explore the idea of Britain in a global world. These range from the preference to avoid further integrationist initiatives, to the renegotiation of the essential character of the relationship between Britain and the EU, together with complete withdrawal. In relation to examining the necessity for the UK to distance itself from ongoing EU integrationalist trends, then Chapter 5 considers the euro as a flawed currency area being a potential key driver to this decision. The reasons are varied for these fundamental flaws: the eurozone fails to fulfil the optimum convergence criteria agreed to be the minimum requirement for the efficient operation of a monetary union; it lacks an adjustment mechanism to meet inevitably changing economic circumstances; its governing institutions, the European Central Bank (ECB) and the European Commission (EC), are not subject to democratic accountability; it was adopted for essentially non-economic motives as the next stage of an integrationist European project, but without the necessary political coordination to underpin it. Hence, the connection between the operation of the euro and the recent worldwide economic recession illustrates the key theme of this book, that national self-governance offers the potential for superior economic performance.

This argument is extended in Chapters 6 and 7 that outline alternative relationships between Britain and the EU. Firstly, we explore how loosening the ties that bind could be undertaken short of complete withdrawal. The evidence presented in previous chapters demonstrates that, on balance, EU membership, and the momentum towards further political and economic integration, has tended to weaken UK national interests. However, it makes little sense to allow a nation's democratic self-determination to be undermined through participation in further initiatives leading towards deeper economic and political integration without first considering a range of alternatives that exist for the UK, and that may facilitate more economic prosperity coupled with enhanced democratic accountability via the national parliament. Hence, Chapter 6 outlines a number of these policy options and evaluates their potential. The first of these is the status quo position, which is the most obvious alternative short-term position, whereby the UK retains EU membership but relies upon its opt-outs from EMU and refuses to participate in further economic and political integration. A second option is to press for renegotiation of the obligations posed by EU membership, together with the ability to opt-out from specific policy initiatives that would have the potential to resolve many of the issues that have generated the greatest costs for the British economy. A more novel approach involves the creation of an Associated European Area (AEA), which would provide a distinctive choice in the type of European integration and pan-national, regional collaboration. A third strategy would involve the UK re-joining the European Free Trade Association (EFTA) that it helped found four decades ago, whilst in the process, it would be eligible for membership of the European Economic Area (EEA). Finally, one further option that the British government could consider relates to formal withdrawal from full EU membership and its replacement with a bilateral trade agreement between the EU and UK.

This final alternative of withdrawal might appear radical and so Chapter 7 discusses the idea of Britain outside the EU in depth. Although leading British political figures have argued for a loosening of the constraints imposed upon nation states by the integration process and both Conservative and Labour governments have drawn their 'red lines' or vetoed specific new initiatives usually seeking to limit national self-determination, the process of ever-closer unification has progressed from the trade-related common market to the establishment of EMU. Consequently, withdrawal from the EU provides one means of escaping these increasing constraints imposed by the EU upon the UK's economic behaviour, and which are not fully eliminated by those options involving retained EU membership. Once achieved, the UK can develop whatever trading relations with other nations it desires; for example, taking advantage of the lower tariffs predominating in the world economy due to successive trade agreements. Or it can make alternative trade alliances; possibly rejoining the European Free Trade Association (EFTA), or even reinvigorating the Commonwealth trading bloc. A third alternative is to form an association with the North American Free Trade Agreement (NAFTA). Approximately one quarter of UK trade is already done with the USA, this bloc, together with the Commonwealth link to Canada, would be beneficial for the UK.

The cost-benefit analysis of withdrawal is explored in order to try and ascertain whether this option is realistic or would have too great a cost, as is claimed by supporters of the integrationist project. The viability of the withdrawal option is important because the bargaining position relating to any renegotiation of EU treaties will not be taken seriously without this ultimate 'threat'. If the EU really is the only option, then loosening the organisation may not be advisable or even practically realisable. However, if independence is proven to have considerable potential for policy innovation, at little or no economic or political cost, then this changes the balance of the argument significantly.

The final section of the book, therefore, explores potential options for a more independent UK through considering what economic, social and political frameworks might look like in these new circumstances. Would a greater (or complete) degree of independence from the EU facilitate economic development? Would it enable more sophisticated economic policy innovation and improved macroeconomic balance as a result? Would social and employment policy be better delivered at national rather than federal level? Is it possible for independence to deliver protection for employees without unduly burdening (small) business? Could independence revitalise the democratic process in Britain? Might the reassertion of parliamentary sovereignty and national self-determination deliver net benefits for UK citizens?

Chapter 8 therefore considers the first of the potential options for a new economic policy framework through outlining a number of broad alternative economic strategies together with the development of complementary industrial strategy and exchange rate policy. The first potential economic strategy seeks to follow the framework whereby national monetary authorities seek a higher long-term growth rate by providing a favourable climate for industrial expansion through low inflation and hence reduced long-term interest rates. Fiscal policy is used to support the more dominant monetary policy by restraining inflationary pressures, thereby reinforcing the low interest rate objective. A second distinctive economic strategy involves the more active use of fiscal as well as monetary policy in order to pursue a mixture of demand-side reflation and supply-side labour market policies. Thus, the net stimulative effect is targeted upon specific sectors of the economy that most require assistance, rather than raising aggregate demand *per se* and creating inflationary bottlenecks.

Given that a distinctive feature of the model advanced by the EU concerns the creation of a social dimension to counter-balance the less desirable consequences likely to arise from the unfettered operation of free market forces, then Chapter 9 addresses the issue of a new social policy framework once outside the EU. The preferred European Social Model (ESM) is typically presented with little consideration of its plausibility and internal coherence, however, there is little critical analysis exploring whether the creation and maintenance of an ESM is consistent with other elements of the European project. Hence, this chapter concentrates upon the potential for the establishment of a successful ESM, and whether this endeavour contradicts and conflicts with the broader drift of European integration.

As the previous chapters have demonstrated, the European project has profound implications for social, political and economic aspects of national life. This is certainly the case in terms of the development of national, sovereign, democratic self-determination, thus in Chapter 10 we seek to develop a new political sovereignty framework. However, reticence to discuss issues of sovereignty have frequently derived from the observation that a majority of British citizens remain suspicious of the European 'project' and oppose the gradual erosion of their rights of self-government. Indeed, it would appear reasonable to conclude that there has long been a historical tendency on behalf of the political class to blur the issues when discussing the implications for sovereignty and self-determination arising from UK participation in the EU.

Essentially, this book asks whether the UK is truly *Moored to the Continent?* Whether this is inevitable, or whether alternatives exist which have the potential to deliver real economic, social and political benefits to the nation? It is hoped that the contents of this book provide some answers to these questions and may stimulate a wider debate on this vital policy question, and thereby inform future policy initiatives towards the EU.

CHAPTER 2

THE MYTH OF GLOBALISATION AND ECONOMIC INTERDEPENDENCE

Introduction

One of the most influential arguments in favour of continued European integration relates to the assertion that an increased internationalisation, or globalisation, of the world economy has created a new environment that has eroded the efficiency of traditional policy instruments and with it the relevance of individual nation states. This partially derives from conceptions of a 'borderless world' (Ohmae, 1990; Naisbitt, 1994), within which 'the stateless corporation' operates, relocating the location of production facilities with relative ease on the basis of calculations that optimise profits and productivity (Holstein, 1990; Reich, 1992). Simultaneously, technological advances have produced cost reductions in transport and communications and facilitated the development of a light, information-knowledge-based, service-centred economy (Katz, 1988; Carnoy *et al.*, 1993; Castells, 1996).

The combination of these developments, further facilitated by a (quarter of a century) shift towards liberalisation of markets amongst most major economies, has given rise to a hyper-globalisation thesis. This claims that the integration of financial markets, the free movement of capital and the rising importance of Trans-National Corporations (TNCs) in global manufacturing production, and their use of Foreign Direct Investment (FDI) to expand their control into an increasing number of national markets, has undermined the abilities of nation states to successfully manage their own affairs (Ohmae, 1990; 1993; 1995; Reich, 1992; Hay, 1999). It is further suggested that the authority of national governments has 'leaked away, upwards, sideways, and downwards', with states being 'hollowed out' by a combination of ease of evasion of regulation and dramatic increases in capital mobility (Cerny, 1990; Strange, 2000).

This conclusion is particularly problematic for progressive, more naturally interventionist political forces, as achievement of traditional priorities has typically been associated with the utilisation of a 'strong' state apparatus (Perraton *et al.*, 2000; Daniels, 2003). Indeed, Favretto (2003:136) has suggested that European integration is 'the only framework within which the European Left can have a future', whilst Sassoon (1999:35–6) claimed that the demise of European regional integration 'would foreshadow the dissolution of the European Left in any recognisable shape'. However, irrespective of the political dimension, European integration is presented as a potential solution to the dilution of national autonomy resulting from these changes.

There is an inherent contradiction within this standpoint, however, as regional integration represents both a response towards, and expression of, globalisation (Vandenbroucke, 1996; Giddens, 2002), and hence advocates differ wildly as to the reasons for this conclusion. One standpoint argues that regional integration represents an intermediate step upon the road towards full globalisation (Tober, 1993; Hettne, 1994). Support for further and deeper integration will, according to this viewpoint, more rapidly complete the globalisation project. However, in sharp contrast, another body of thought proposes that the EU offers the possibility to rediscover former state influence within a larger super-national entity, less open to the vagaries of financial market speculation and changes in trade patterns since a larger proportion of economic activity occurs within the EU single market than applies to each individual member states from which it is comprised. Accordingly, government policy instruments are more effective when wielded at the federal level. This could be manifested in an outward-facing, euro-Keynesian regionally co-ordinated reflation strategy, of the type advocated in the 1980s, and revisited in 1991 by the EU Commission under Delors (Callaghan, 2000). Alternatively, it could lead towards an insular, neo-protectionist 'Fortress Europe'-type approach (Scholte, 2000), emphasising unique aspects of the 'European Social Model' (this topic is further explored in Chapter 9). In either case, it has been suggested that an increasingly integrated Europe provides 'the only force capable of countervailing the sovereignty of the global market-place' (Marquand, 1999:15).

This chapter, therefore, offers a brief resume of these arguments and offers insights as to how the hyper-globalisation thesis is largely incorrect in its more far-reaching conclusions.

Globalisation — a contested concept

Globalisation is quite possibly 'the most contested concept in contemporary social science' (Grant, 2002:41), being 'invariably over-used and under-specified' (Higgott and Payne, 2000:ix). Indeed, the imprecision that often accompanies debate surrounding globalisation prompted Wiseman (1998:1) to claim it to be 'the most slippery, dangerous and important buzzword of the late twentieth century', and beyond.

At its most narrow, globalisation refers to an evolving pattern of cross-border activities of firms involving international investment, trade and collaboration for purposes of product development, production, sourcing and marketing. It involves an increasing flow of goods, services, technology and capital across national borders. The OECD (1996:9) describes it as an 'evolving pattern of cross-border activities of firms involving international investment, trade and collaboration for purposes of product, development, production and sourcing and marketing'. On a micro level, Ruigrok and van Tulder (1995) discuss globalisation in terms of corporate strategies to establish a global intra-firm, in addition to inter-firm, division of labour. However, the fact that the present international system is characterised by a relatively high degree of interdependence amongst nations and societies, when measured in historical terms, is, however, an *insufficient* definition of globalisation.

A broader and more accurate definition incorporates both the internationalisation of economic production and capital flows, the growing dominance of FDI and TNCs, together with a cultural aspect which embraces varying currents of global branding (Nike, MacDonalds, Coca-Cola) and a tension between 'westernisation' and an increase in national (and sub-national) cultural identity (Hirst and Thompson, 1996; Scholte, 2000; Whyman, 2007). These phenomena are often linked with discussion of an 'information society', where the power and cost-effectiveness of communication has increased exponentially, and this facilitates the growth of global markets for products, specialised labour and especially financial assets (Giddens and Hutton, 2000). The low cost of communications and transportation, as a proportion of the total cost of goods and services, facilitates the geographical diversification of corporation production, whilst the 'weightless economy' further exacerbates these trends (Rustin, 2001:18).

Globalisation, then, relates to the multiplicity of interconnections between nations and societies, and describes the means by which phenomena occurring in one area of the globe impact upon the activities of individuals in a geographically distinct region. It therefore involves a spatial linkage, together with an intensification and interdependence between nations and social groupings. Globalisation produces a re-configeration of geography, causing social space to be defined in terms distinct from territorial places and independent of national borders (Scholte, 2000). It incorporates the growth of international consumer markets in cultural, as well as consumer, products. Finally, the globalisation thesis infers a reduced role for national government policy, and an increased potential for surpranational economic regulation (McGrew and Lewis, 1992).

Evidence

Certain facts are uncontested. Thus, between 1970 and 1991, world GDP doubled, global exports nearly tripled in real terms and FDI quadrupled, with rates of real increase exceeding 25 per cent per annum during the latter half of the 1980s (UNCTAD, 1993:17). Moreover, it is estimated that the largest 500 TNCs perform a majority of world trade (UNCTAD, 1995), with a handful of firms dominating in such diverse markets as telecommunications, semiconductors, consumer durables, air travel, accountancy services, global news provision, credit cards, the recorded music industry, steel, automobile and oil production (Whyman, 2006). Indeed, the 15 largest TNCs have each produced annual sales figures exceeding the GDP of over 120 nations. Moreover, alongside increases in FDI, there has been a substantial surge in foreign portfolio investment, taking the ratio of foreign assets relative to world GDP from 17.7 per cent in 1980 to 56.8 per cent in 1995 (Crafts, 2000). However, the most spectacular evidence for globalisation relates to the extraordinary expansion in short-term financial capital flows, with figures traded on the major foreign exchange markets approaching one hundred times the equivalent value of international trade and dwarfing the total world expenditure on crude oil (Eatwell, 2000; Helleiner, 2000). One estimate suggests that derivatives trading alone accounts for more than twelve times global GDP (Castells, 2000). Thus, the vast majority of financial market transactions are speculative in nature, and have no relation to the real economy, reversing the situation in 1971, when 90 per cent of all financial transactions were made to facilitate international trade and long-term productive investment (Eatwell, 1995; Watson, 2002).

Is globalisation new?

The fact that the world economy has experienced a dramatic internationalisation does not, however, imply that these events are necessarily unique or have the consequences suggested by the more ardent advocates of globalisation. Indeed, proportionally at least, levels of international trade, migration of labour and international flows of investment capital, were higher in the late nineteenth century than the comparable situation at the end of the twentieth century (Wade, 1996). One description of globalisation during the gold standard time period has a remarkably contemporary feel;

> What an extraordinary episode in the economic progress of man that age was which came to an end in August 1914...the inhabitant of London could order by telephone, supping his morning tea in bed, the various products of the whole earth, in such quantity as he might see fit, and reasonably expect their early delivery upon his doorstep; he could at the same moment and by the same means adventure his wealth in the natural resources and new enterprises of any quarter of the world and share, without exertion or even trouble, in their prospective fruits and advantages ... He could secure forthwith, if he wished it, cheap and comfortable means of transit to any country or climate without passport or other formality, could dispatch his servant to the neighbouring office of a bank for such supply of the precious metals as might seem convenient, and could then proceed abroad to foreign quarters, without knowledge of their religion, language or customs, bearing coined wealth upon his person, and would consider himself most greatly aggrieved and much surprised at the least interference. But, most important of all, he regarded this state of affairs as normal, certain and permanent. (Keynes, 1920:10–12).

In terms of international trade, the UK's trade as a proportion of GDP was at a similar level in 1913 as at the beginning of the twenty-first century, with France and Japan recording lower levels of trade openness (Hirst and Thompson, 1996). Capital mobility amongst the leading industrial nations also appears to be lower today than almost a century previously (Hirst and Thompson, 1996; Obstfeld and Taylor, 1997). Consequently, whilst the trends of the last two decades have resulted in significant changes in the international economy, these are not without precedent. Indeed, it is plausible to describe the process of internationalisation as a recurrent historical trend, complete with alternating phases of globalisation and fragmentation that has been repeated on a number of occasions in the history of the modern nation state (Clark, 1997).

Globalisation and the decline of the nation state?

The evidence for an increase in international economic interconnectedness does not, by itself, prove the globalisation thesis, because much of the available data can arguably sustain distinct claims of internationalisation and/or regionalisation of economies (Vandenbroucke, 1996). In this context, internationalisation may be associated with the documented expansion of international trade and portfolio investment capital flows. However, its distinctive feature is that principal economic units remain essentially national (Hirst and Thompson, 1996; Petrella, 1996). In contrast, globalisation involves the transformation of production, as TNCs lose their former national identity, become truly footloose in terms of location of production and their international management owes no residual allegiance to the interests of any individual nation state.

Globalisation, therefore, would be associated with 'macroeconomic unification' (Glyn and Sutcliffe, 1992:77) as governments find it difficult (if not impossible) to control global TNCs and thus the international economic system becomes relatively autonomous, subject only to minimal international regulation (Hirst and Thompson, 1996). This is associated in the literature with a predicted decline in the ability of the nation state to determine its own economic policies (Ohmae, 1995; Strange, 1996).

Capital mobility

One aspect of this postulated weakening of state power relates to the fact that financial deregulation has provided additional *exit options* for private capital. Corporations can relocate more easily than in the past, and hence governments may not find it as easy to tax more mobile assets as highly as previously. It is not a large step to move towards a system of global tax competition, where corporations threaten to relocate unless governments reduce their tax burdens, or provide them with a variety of subsidies (i.e. rent rebates, provision of 'greenfield' sites for development and infrastructural investment) predominantly benefiting the company but financed by tax-payers. Similarly, nation states may use tax competition as one incentive to attract FDI, thereby further driving down tax revenues (eg. Ireland, Germany).

This has to be qualified by the fact that, for most industrialised economies, total FDI flows represent only a small proportion of GDP and are exceeded by domestic investment by at least a factor of nine-to-one (Weiss, 1998). For many nations, including Britain, outward flows exceed inward investment, such that renewed regulation of long-term investment, in addition to controls over short-term capital flows, might benefit certain nations. Moreover, the fact remains that 81 per cent of global FDI stock is located in high wage, high tax OECD nations, indicating that cost reduction is not the overwhelming factor causing the globalisation of production (Weiss, 1998). TNCs typically concentrate around three-quarters of value-adding activities in their home nation, indicating that they are more accurately 'national firms which operate internationally whilst retaining a home base' and not the 'footloose' firms as so often depicted (Wade, 1996:101; Hirst and Thompson, 1996:96). Indeed, it is paradoxically the greater potential for physical capital mobility that places a greater importance upon the physical infrastructure, access to affluent markets and technology, together with the skill and commitment of the workforce that have become increasingly important in determining a company or nation's competitive position, and which are themselves relatively immobile factors (Dunning, 1988; Wade, 1996).

The 'embeddedness of companies in national institutions' provides information and a means of co-ordination between firms to secure common objectives, facilitates the development of a cluster of skilled labour and a technical supply chain specialising in the specific activity of the firm, thereby reducing the uncertainty arising from a dynamic business environment (Zysman, 2000:120–23). This can arise from:

1. New technologies place a premium on fixed costs (i.e. equipment, machinery, etc.) whilst reducing the importance of variable costs (wages, raw materials). Indeed certain types of labour (especially knowledge-intensive labour) tend to be treated increasingly as a fixed cost. The general effect of this transformation, most notably in the highly developed countries, is to reduce the cost savings to be gained by moving to low-income sites.
2. Many new production methods emphasize the growing importance of physical proximity between producers and suppliers (especially in non-assembly operations). Such methods tend to privilege local supplier networks, thus providing a counter-trend towards the constitution of regional rather than global sourcing networks.
3. Domestic linkages—national institutional frameworks—enmesh business in support relationships with trade associations, training and financial institutions, and national and local governments.

Consequently, a 'national system of innovation' can be extremely successful in developing international competitive advantage (Porter, 1990; Patel and Pavitt, 1991).

Tax pressure

Trans-national production additionally provides the opportunity for tax avoidance through the mechanism of transfer pricing, which involves the prices of inter-firm transfers of services and materials being manipulated, so that resources are transferred from subsidiaries located in high tax areas and towards sister companies in lower tax regimes. The US Congress found that half of the forty firms it surveyed had paid virtually no taxation over the previous decade (Dicken, 1992). In the boom year of 1987, 59 per cent of foreign owned companies reported no profits in the USA and therefore paid no taxation, whilst these same firms enjoyed a 50 per cent increase in revenue over a three year period and yet tax payments rose by only 2 per cent (Barnet and Kavanagh, 1994).

This evidence is not, however, as definitive as it first may appear. For example, Rodrik (1996) notes that comparable tax rates still vary widely across the industrialised nations, whilst the evidence used to predict convergence is, at best, limited. Eichengreen (1990) notes that the variability of state tax rates remains significant even in an integrated economy such as the USA, albeit at a little over half the level between EU nation states. Indeed, far from those economies that are the most integrated into the world economy suffering a 'shrinkage' of government, there is actually a positive correlation between openness and the share of government expenditure in GDP, due to the ability of government to act as an insulator against external shocks (Kopits, 1992; Rodrik, 1996). Moreover, it has, for example, not led to the collapse of the welfare state nor forced tax levels to a common, low level. Though marginal corporation taxes have in many cases been reduced, this has been typically balanced by a broadening of the tax base through the closure of loopholes Swank (1998). Therefore, it would appear from the available data that, even where capital taxation may be squeezed because of increased mobility, this is not so dramatic as headline rates may suggest, whilst the potential for significant variation is likely to remain.

Crisis of the state

A third issue concerns the argument that trans-nationalisation of the economic environment reduces the economic space left to be controlled by the nation state. Susan Strange (1994) discussed this phenomenon in terms of a 'hollowing' of state authority and a 'retreat of the state'. For example, nation states are increasingly being forced to bargain with TNCs over their conditions of operation, rather than regulate their activities (Stopford and Strange, 1991). Regulation becomes difficult when corporations can avoid constraints through relocation or internal transfers of resources. Thus, governments may fall back upon the regulation of labour and ease restrictions on capital, with the inevitable negative distributional consequences.

This portrayal, however, neglects the fact that markets are not natural phenomena, but are always established in some form of legal and institutional context that defines the conditions under which transactions occur. Ultimately, the power of the nation state creates the conditions for markets to operate, for example, by creating legal protection for most transactions, employing inspection teams to ensure the integrity of the trade (i.e. checking weights and measures, the accuracy of advertising, and the safety of the product or service). If nation states were not complicit in the sanctioning of offshore financial centres, by providing legal protection of their trades with on-shore individuals and organisations, this evasion of regulation would be greatly curtailed. Moreover, whilst innovation, aided by developments in information technology, may facilitate intelligent avoidance of national regulation, these same factors could just as easily be utilised by a determined sovereign state to devise new controls intended to benefit and stabilise the real economy.

Increased cost of national policies

A fourth topic relates to manner in which global financial markets increase the cost of domestic stabilization policies (Kapstein, 1994). Accordingly, it is suggested that there has been a shift away from *welfare* states to *competition* states, as active fiscal policy is discouraged by financial markets, as these prefer low rates of taxation and mildly deflationary policies as this preserves the value of financial assets (Reich, 1992; Palley, 1999). Unless governments are prepared to regulate financial markets to reduce their influence over macroeconomic policy, policy makers will come under increasing pressure to design policy programmes that command confidence in the financial markets rather than what is in the long-term interest of the real economy, as these two interests are often not synonymous (Gill, 1998). Cerny (1990; 1997) argues that the nation state is forced to consider the interests of mobile capital in order to increase its attractiveness as a location for production, hence reducing the burden of business taxation, emphasis upon neo-liberal economic policies and engaging in 'regulatory arbitrage' to create conditions more attractive to mobile capital. Similarly, social policy is redesigned to reinforce labour market policies rather than decommodify citizens (Jessop, 1993; 1994).

This aspect can, however, be over-emphasised. For example, many market-liberal economists would perceive no negative impact in increased international competition pressuring governments to reduce spending and liberalise their economies. Keynesian economists would view such developments as disadvantageous for smooth periods of economic development, yet these trends are as yet weak in their effects. Nation states retain control over monetary policy, certainly within the range of normal policy parameters, as evidenced by the absence of a global rate of interest, varied only by differential risk factors in individual nation states; this being a defining feature of complete financial market integration. Yet, even where financial integration has occurred, benefits in terms of economies of scale and innovation have to be set alongside the increased probability of contagion from financial crises elsewhere in the international community. Crises have caused shock waves rippling out of events in Mexico, Russia, South East Asia, Argentina, Brazil and currently a credit crisis emanating from USA, due largely to a substantial increase in short-term liquidity through financial capital flows, combined with over-exposure to innovative but high risk financial instruments, spreading to the domestic economy (Kapstein, 1994). This may weaken state power, but might also caution against closer integration in the absence of sufficiently tight supranational regulation to prevent occurrences of this kind and thereby reinforce calls for the re-regulation of national economies.

Advocates of participation in the European EMU have argued that this is necessary to prevent the destabilisation caused by fluctuations in variable currencies and/or the impact of speculation undermining traditional models of fixed exchange rates. The ERM crisis in the early 1990s is often used as an example of why EMU is necessary and why national currencies are vulnerable to the vagaries of global financial flows. However, these same events reinforce both the limitations to this argument and the continued viability of exchange rate management as a key macroeconomic policy instrument. It was the mistaken decision to fix sterling's value within the ERM at a rate higher than that required to maintain international competitiveness—the rationale being that this would discipline the economy and provide downward pressure upon inflation. The resultant recession and rapidly rising unemployment were likely consequences of this decision, whilst the subsequent economic recovery was equally predictable following the (forced) devaluation of the currency and exit from the constraints imposed by the European exchange rate system (Burkitt *et al.*, 1996; Baimbridge *et al.*, 2005).

Furthermore, there remain a plethora of different exchange rate systems, ranging from the Euro-single currency, to fixed exchange regimes (i.e. ERM), currency baskets, adjustable (crawling) pegs, managed and free floating. Thus, far from the state being powerless, it actually retains substantial capacities to govern global economic activities (Boyer and Drache, 1996; Weiss, 1998).

Viable national economic management

There is additionally little convincing evidence to indicate that globalisation has undermined the efficiency of institutional frameworks within which economic policy operates (Garrett, 1995). Careful examination of the data leads a number of theorists to conclude that contemporary phenomenon relates more closely to internationalisation than globalisation (Hirst and Thompson, 1996; Wade, 1996). It is a misunderstanding, then, as Panitch (1994) states, that globalisation equals the end of the nation state and the constraints upon national policy are exaggerated. Indeed, it is perhaps worth noting that claims of 'the end of the nation state' have coincided with more nation states existing than during any previous historical period of world history. National macroeconomics remains a viable alternative for any nation to pursue (Baker *et al.*, 2002). Nation states remain essentially sovereign; influenced by the international economy, certainly, and with their freedom of movement constrained by the consequences of specific actions, naturally, yet remaining sufficiently autonomous to devise and implement a distinctive, self-determined economic strategy tailored to the needs of its economy and preferences of its electorate.

But what should that national economic policy resemble? Should it draw inspiration from the low tax, deregulated, neo-liberal market-orientated economics, or alternatively adopt a more interventionist, active macroeconomic policy evolving from Keynesian principles? This debate is considered in more detail in Chapter 8. However, for here, it is sufficient to note that this is the type of debate that should inform the design of a national economic programme, with the result being determined by a combination of the superiority of ideas and democratic will of the majority of citizens, rather than being stymied by the over-exaggerated claims of the hyper-globalists that would dismiss the relevance of any such discourse.

CHAPTER 3

BRITAIN AND THE EU
SO CLOSE YET SO FAR

Introduction

This chapter provides an overview of the historical relationship between the UK and the EU. Firstly, it summarises why the EU is a distinctive entity compared to the other international organisations to which Britain is aligned (e.g. NATO, UN, IMF etc.). It is from this perspective of the unique interrelationship between Britain and the EU that many, if not all, of the tensions emanate from. Secondly, we briefly review the turbulent 'on-off' relationship that characterised the post World War II period. We follow the assessment of Harrison (1996) that the relationship has processed through several distinct phases. Significant for this book overall, the most recent of these can be traced back to the 1988 Bruges speech of Mrs Thatcher and formalised under the leadership William Hague in 1997. The victory of the eurosceptic wing of the Conservative Party over the europhile camp, represented by Kenneth Clarke in the 1997 leadership election, has developed to the point where UK membership is being openly questioned. Thirdly, we examine the potential causes for the often fractious relationship between Britain and its continental neighbours. Possible reasons for this include the UK's unbroken history, the legacy of empire and war, the presence of a distinctive legal system, unique capitalist structure and an individualistic culture. It is argued that these play an important role in contributing to the frequently conflicting aspirations of both people and politicians on each side of the English Channel.

A short history of European integration

The EU is a unique institution, which is continually evolving in bursts of activity interspersed with relative passivity. The intention to peacefully integrate European economies has precedents as far back as the fourteenth century, although the particular form taken by the EU is largely determined by its emergence out of the period of political and economic reconstruction following World War II. Its aim, as specified in the founding 1957 Treaty of Rome, has been to 'lay the foundations of an ever closer union amongst the peoples of Europe and by pooling resources ... to preserve and strengthen peace and liberty'. Thus, the EU was established as a political organisation to enhance security through mutual reconstruction, whilst avoiding excessive nationalism so recently exhibited by European nation states.

From the beginning, the EU has evolved principally through the promotion of economic co-operation and integration preceding ever-closer political ties. Thus, it was foundered through a merger of the European Coal and Steel Community, the European Atomic Energy Community and the European Economic Community. Subsequently, it created a customs union before further integration established a single internal market. Indeed, the creation of EMU between twelve EU member states should be perceived as another step on this road of further integration. However, the principal reason why the architects of this 'new' Europe have preferred economic integration to precede political union is the result of a political conflict between competing visions of the mechanism(s) of achieving closer ties between nations.

Throughout the development of the EU there have been disagreements and fluctuating alliances between federalists, advocating the replacement of individual nation states by a larger democratic structure, internationalists, preferring a global not regional focus, and nationalists, who prefer a community of nation states engaged in free trade. As a result, it has typically been easier to reform trading relations between member states than generate unanimity on more politically sensitive issues such as tax harmonisation, border controls, together with the establishment of a unified army, foreign policy and police force.

The organisational model adopted by the EU reflects its creation as a 'cold war' entity, dominated by Europe's political and business elite. It is the EU Commission, civil servants who *initiate* topics for discussion and provide subsequent drafts of propose legislation, who are thereby able to influence the future agenda. The Council of Ministers comprises representatives of national governments, whose agreement is required for proposals to become legally binding Directives. Thus, the future framework of the EU is determined between two self-selected groups, which are substantially more open to lobbying by business interests than by civic groups (Balanyá *et al.* 2000). The third EU institution, the European Parliament is comprised of directly elected representatives in approximate proportion to a nation's relative population size. However, parliament is a relatively new phenomenon, grafted onto the existing elite model to enhance popular support of the EU institutions whilst simultaneously countering claims of a democratic deficit at the heart of the organisation. Although able to review proposals, the parliament can only affect most issues through the power of its persuasion, with the twin exceptions being the power to reject the annual budget and the ability to sack the entire Commission. Thus, the EU organisational model still suffers from a democratic deficit in terms of direct influence afforded to European citizens over the decision-making process of the principle institutions.

Thus, the main impetus for the formation of a co-operative movement amongst countries in Western Europe was the experience of World War II. Indeed, the need to avert further conflicts and consolidate peace is a goal that the process of European integration has certainly helped to achieve alongside the role of NATO, which should not be underestimated. The first initiative, drawn up by Jean Monnet, the head of the French Commission for Economic Planning, was to ensure that reconstruction in the heavy industries of West Germany should not endanger peace. The result was the European Coal and Steel Treaty (ECST) in 1951, which had three key objectives. Firstly, to ensure integration through the removal of customs duties and quotas over a five year transition period, modernisation and expansion of these industries through investment, the restriction of protectionist state aids and the provision of a common external commercial policy. Secondly, such detailed agreements were subservient to the political goal of achieving stability between France and Germany. Finally, the Treaty was instrumental in setting up supra-national institutions (e.g. the Council of Ministers and European Court of Justice), which would begin the process of closer co-operation between European partners. For her part, Germany was more than happy to accept the possibility of regaining control over its key industries as well as the prospect of rehabilitation, whilst the French, who largely engineered this initiative, along with Belgium, Italy, Luxembourg and the Netherlands also warmly received the proposals. More importantly, this agreement would also come to represent the first tentative steps toward European integration (Baimbridge *et al.*, 2004).

Six years later the European Economic Community (EEC) Treaty was ratified, which laid the foundations for a Common Market for the free movement in services and factors of production and the nurturing of free competition. In 1968, the six original members made further advances by the blanket removal of intra-community trade tariffs, the formation of a common external tariff (CET) on trade with third parties and the adoption of a common commercial policy. The EEC Treaty continued to follow the supra-nationalist model employed in the ECST by creating a framework within which these institutions could more effectively enact EEC legislation and law pertaining to the principles of the single market. However, almost twenty years passed until further steps in European integration materialised in the form of the Single European Act (1986). This legislature would contribute significantly to the integration process through the introduction of qualified majority voting (QMV).[1]

In the 1990s, the objectives of European integration broadened from that of a European Community to a European Union (EU). In the Treaty on European Union (TEU) (commonly known as the Maastricht Treaty) in 1992, three pillars of European decision-making were formalised. The first pillar was essentially the European Community involving the adoption, modification and implementation of a legislative framework for the operation of the single market. The ethos behind the second and third pillars was to encourage intergovernmental co-operation in the areas of Foreign and Security Policy, and Justice and Home Affairs respectively.[2] In this context, the role of the Commission and the European Parliament is limited, where decision-making is made on the basis of Member State representatives in the forum of the Council of Ministers. The EU was, however, still faced with the cumbersome procedure of having to ratify important international agreements with third countries both in the capacity of a single body and as a collection of member states (Baimbridge *et al.*, 2004).

Accordingly, a key feature of the Treaty of Amsterdam in 1997 was to ordain the Council with powers to represent the EU thus providing a more focused point of reference on the world stage. This Treaty also shifted matters pertaining to external border controls, immigration and asylum from the third to the first pillar in an attempt to solidify the concept that full implementation of a single market required a working space that protected the rights and provided security for both EU and non-EU citizens alike. The other major achievement in the 1990s (within the TEU) was the formalisation of guiding principles and mechanisms for Economic and Monetary Union (EMU), which would eventually lead to the adoption of a single currency (Baimbridge *et al.*, 2004).

The other notable development over this fifty year time frame has been the growth in EU stature on the world stage as membership in the original club of six has expanded, beginning with Denmark, Ireland and the United Kingdom joining in 1973. Enlargement to the 'South' previously had been deemed inconceivable due to the political affiliations of the ruling parties. Indeed, up until the early to mid-1970s, Greece, Portugal and Spain were governed by a non-elected body, which was considered as an unofficial (until TEU formalised this requirement) obstacle to entry. However, with the return of democracy, each sought and gained membership throughout the 1980s, starting with Greece (1981) followed by Portugal and Spain (1986). Finally, in 1996, the EU enlarged again with the accessions of Austria, Finland and Sweden. In 2004, the Union embraced another 10 members: Cyprus, the Czech Republic, Estonia, Hungary, Latvia, Lithuania, Malta, Poland, Slovakia, Slovenia; with Bulgaria and Romania following in 2007. Further enlargements are to be expected, as Croatia has already applied for Candidate status whilst a number of western Balkan states (Albania, Bosnia-Herzegovina, Macedonia, Serbia, Montenegro) are each aspiring for membership over the coming years, not forgetting the long-standing position of Turkey as an aspirant member.

Why the EU is distinctive

Prior to examining in detail the historical relationship between Britain and the EU, the unique aspects of the features of the EU that make it a distinctive entity need to be reviewed. Firstly, the scale of the EU's activities and its impact on British life is illustrated by its geographical reach, population and trading capacity. However, it can also be viewed through the extent of EU policy competences. From an organisation originally designed to promote competition and trade, has developed a wide range of policy responsibilities, whilst EMU and the attempt to introduce a Constitution has moved the EU closer to actual statehood. Even the policy areas where national governments have guarded their sovereignty (e.g. foreign policy and justice issues) have become the subject of increasing supranational collaboration. Secondly, the EU comprises a complex set of institutional structures and policy arrangements. Thirdly, it is unlike most supranational organizations (where relationships are mediated through national governments) in the extent to which the EU seeks a progressively more direct relationship with the civil societies and citizens of its member states. For example, the Treaty of Amsterdam of 1997 made the citizens of member states citizens of the EU, thereby establishing the dual loyalty and identity found in federal systems. Indeed, the EU Constitution represented a further extension in this direction until its derailing by the electorate of France and the Netherlands in 2005. Thus on some measures, the structures of the European Union are already well advanced towards the federal model and display greater integration than those of well-established federations such as the United States (McKay, 1999, 2001).

Finally, the EU is also distinctive amongst international organisations in being able to act autonomously of its national members whereby much EU legislation has direct and immediate effect. Subsidiarity (the principle that decisions should be taken at the lowest possible level) often appears more honoured in the breach than in the observance, and a more powerful dynamic within the EU seems to be one of pushing policy towards the European level of decision-making. Most important of all, perhaps, in giving the EU a distinctive and controversial character is that there is no consensus between its member states regarding its final goal; whether its aim is confederation, federation or simply a closer union of independent nation states (Peele, 2004).

The formal political relationship

The most important source of external influence on British politics since the late 1960s and the UK's first membership application was not a single country but what is now the EU. On the European issue the Liberals (latterly Liberal Democrats) are alone amongst the parties to show consistency, nourished by their distance from power after 1945. In contrast, Labour and Conservative parties have pursued electoral advantage through syncopations of policy over seven broad phases between 1945 and the present (Table 3.1). Harrison (1996) labels the initial six phases as: Conservative Europeanism (1945–51), British isolationism (1951–61), revived Conservative Europeanism (1961–7), all-party Europeanism (1967–70), revived Conservative Europeanism (1970–5), and revived all-party Europeanism (1975–97), which continues for the Labour Party. However, a seventh phase can be identified, namely that of Conservative euroscepticism (1997–).

Table 3.1 Summary of the UK–EU relationship

Phases of UK–EU relationship	Comment
Conservative Europeanism (1945–51)	Winston Churchill demonstrated more sympathy than Labour with Europe's aspirations to unity, but this did not entail any choice between Europe and the 'open seas'.
British	On taking office Churchill disappointed some Conservative

isolationism (1951–61)	'Europeans' by opting clearly for the open seas, thereby launching the second (isolationist) phase.
Revived Conservative Europeanism (1961–7)	The first application for entry in 1961 launched the third phase. Although Britain had at last reached the situation where the government was in favour of membership and Macmillan's bid failed with de Gaulle partly because of the conflict between the low-key domestic campaign he conducted and the need to convince the French that Britain was psychologically 'ready' for the change. Moreover, de Gaulle realised that Macmillan had not abandoned pursuit of the 'special relationship' on defence and other matters with the United States. In Heath, however, the Conservatives found a leader who was 'not inclined to postpone choices, whose instincts on foreign policy were far more radical, and who was ready to use his influence within his Party energetic to push Euro-sceptics into a minority' (Harrison, 1996).
All-party Europeanism (1967–70)	Wilson's application for entry launched the fourth phase, during which for the first time Europeanism encompassed both government and opposition, indeed the Conservatives took the unusual step of imposing a three-line whip in favour of Wilson's decision to apply. However, whilst the leaders in both parties now favoured membership, their rank and file contained dissidents. In particular, Labour dissidents were determined to exploit the European issue as a way of repudiating the Wilson government that had disappointed them on other issues.
Revived Conservative Europeanism (1970–75)	Hence, in the fifth phase, Europeanism reverted to being a single-party alignment. Once in power in 1974 Labour set about restoring all-party agreement on EEC membership, negotiating amended terms of accession, subject to the referendum that emerged as a device for holding its pro- and anti-EEC wings together. The two-to-one referendum victory placed Labour's eurosceptic left on the defensive such that party activists, who prided themselves on being more closely in touch with opinion than the leaders they criticized, received a severe shock.
Revived all-party Europeanism (1975–97)	Although both Labour and Conservative governments saw themselves as European throughout this phase, both parties were divided. Labour at first remained sufficiently eurosceptic in defence of Britain's continued EEC membership to fuel the SDP's secession. By the summer of 1980 Labour's Europeans were on the defensive, and three

	members of the future 'gang of four' (Williams, Owen, and Rodgers) issued a statement deploring the revived threat to leave the EEC. However, the subsequent party conference ignored David Owen's plea and voted to take Britain out of the EEC without a referendum. On the Conservative side of the political divide, as long as the EEC saw itself as a community of nation states that provided an enlarged free market for British goods, Thatcher had no difficulty with membership. She was able to silence the developing divide in her party after 1979 by her desire to improve the financial basis of Britain's membership in relation to the Community budget. However, two developments in the 1980s made this position difficult to sustain. Firstly, the contrast between a free-market Britain and an interventionist EEC progressively widened under the Thatcher revolution and secondly, whilst the EEC moved from being a free-trade area to economic and then political union. Indeed, by the mid-1980s Labour was becoming more sympathetic to the EEC given that socialism was now on the defensive at home, the EEC began to seem for Labour a last redoubt for these values. Simultaneously, Thatcher was losing a sequence of important ministers (Heseltine, Lawson, and Howe) who disliked the anti-European direction she now seemed to be taking.
Conservative euroscepticism (1997–)	Hence, commencing under the premiership of Thatcher and her 1988 Bruges speech, there has been a discernable drift away from the Heath inspired Europeanisation of the Conservative Party. This was further highlighted by the Treaty on European Union ratification process between December 1991 and July 1993 and elsewhere in the government of John Major (1992–97). However, it was with the leadership of William Hague (1997–2001) that the final rupture in the post-1975 all-party Europeanisation consensus could be most clearly pinpointed. Thus we identify a seventh phase of Conservative euroscepticism of which the seeds had been sown almost a decade prior, but which came to fruition under the leadership of William Hague in 1997. Hague sought to make the EU, and in particular the adoption of the euro, a key issue of difference ('clear blue water' being the catchphrase of the time) between New Labour and the Conservatives. Whilst this caused tensions in his party, it also led to it doubling its seats (to 36) in the 1999 European Parliamentary elections suggesting it to be a popular stance. However, it proved less effective in the 2001 general election when the issue of Europe registered lower than the traditional concerns of the economy, health and

	education etc. However, two leaders later and this distinctive eurosceptical focus remains at the forefront of Conservative policy. Indeed, they fought the 2005 general election with the most eurosceptic manifesto of the three main national parties.

Source: Adapted from Harrison (1996)

The question therefore becomes: what does this seven-fold sequence reveal about the two main political parties? Firstly, because they compete for electoral advantage through seeking new sources of support, full ventilation for eurosceptic and europhile opinion has been assured, even at the expense of party consistency on policy. Secondly, Britain's EU story reveals the importance of divisions within, as well as between, parties in the process of seeking opinion likely to be electorally helpful. Thirdly, although the EU is difficult to fit into the traditions of both Conservative and Labour parties, it did not in itself prompt the emergence of a centre party (although it has arguably led to the rise of the UK Independence Party, ironically aided by the instigation of proportional representation for European Parliament elections) still less an electoral system favouring centrist government. Indeed, the two-party system has been tenacious enough to survive continuous comparison with the proportional representation and centre-government coalition systems in the EU. Fourthly, there is the two-party system's capacity to present an image of indecision, inconsistency, and even bad faith. This has done nothing to boost Britain's reputation within the EU, though such wavering and hesitation probably accurately reflects the state of British opinion on the issue since the 1950s.

This raises the rather different question of how public opinion on the European issue has impinged on the political system since 1945. Harrison (1996) argues that pressure groups directly concerned with the matter have been relatively unimportant. Interest and cause groups concerned with specific areas of policy, gravitating as they instinctively do to the centres of power, have of course been active at the European level. Yet Britain's three applications to join the (then) EEC did not result from pressure-group activity. Thus, if pressure groups were relatively unimportant, why did public opinion not only accept that Britain should not only enter the (then) EEC, but also the steady extension of its aspirations? The answer is that general public have seldom been overtly enlisted in the process. There has been only one referendum, whilst general elections have never centred upon the European issue, bar perhaps the one-sided attempt by Hague in 2001.

Although the 1975 referendum did at least involve the public in reaching a decision, many commentators argue that Wilson's handling of the entire issue since 1970 had loaded the decision in favour of entry and continued membership (Butler and Kitzinger, 1976). However, as previously described, there has been a perceptible rise in euroscepticism both within the major parties and through the emergence of smaller parties such as the UK Independence Party and the Green Party of England and Wales. Hence, public disenchantment with the EU has begun to find specific outlets (voice) within the political arena.

Reasons for British difficulties with the EU

There is both a scholarly and a political debate about why Britain has so often appeared to be at odds with its European neighbours (George, 1992, 1998). These can be summarised in the frequently expressed questions: Why does Britain not appear to share the vision of the other member states? Why does the UK so often resist common policies? Why is it that it always seems to be Britain that wants special treatment? Why in spite of its size and international influence is the British government perceived as trying to block or dilute the impact of initiatives from Brussels? Here we seek to summarise the many and complex reasons for Britain's lack of enthusiasm towards the European project when the rest of Europe seems keen on economic and political integration.

The first theme revolves around the notion of an unbroken history. In particular, this relates to the lack of invasion, absence of revolution and being an 'old' state in a 'new' world. Firstly, given a lack of invasion, it is impossible to understand Britain's place in Europe without appreciating the importance of the institutional continuity of British political structures. Most of continental Europe has been swept by invading armies several times in the past couple of hundred years, but England has not been invaded since 1066. Secondly, there has been an absence of revolution, whereby Britain has not undergone a dramatic revolutionary upheaval, such as those that transformed France (1789) or Russia (1917). The closest was the Civil War (1642–8) and the Glorious Revolution (1689) that established the principle of parliamentary sovereignty and a constitutional monarchy; hence crucially these reformed the institutions of governance rather than replacing them with new ones.

Additional explanation within this theme is the idea of Britain as an old state in a new world, such that when we look at the rest of Europe most states are either relatively new, or have gone through upheavals in the recent past as a result of wars or revolutions. For example, Germany was only unified as a single state in 1870, but it was then divided again in 1945, and was finally reunified as recently as 1990; Spain, Portugal and Greece were under military dictatorships as late as the 1970s, so their contemporary political institutions and structures are relatively new; whilst Yugoslavia came into being after World War I and has since disintegrated into its constituent parts. Moreover, some of the countries who have recently joined the EU (Hungary, Poland and the Czech Republic), have recently been reconstituted following the end of the Russian occupation, and other areas, like the three Baltic states (Latvia, Lithuania and Estonia) have only established their independence since the implosion of the Soviet Union at the start of the 1990s.

A second aspect unique to Britain relates to the twin concepts of empire and war. Here both the legacy of empire and the pretence of global influence are regarded as explanatory causes of Britain's non-alignment with the rest of Europe. Although its empire disappeared in a very short time after the World War II, what the empire left behind, however, was a pattern of international trade and cooperation that looked away from Europe in the guise of the Commonwealth. One of the major considerations when Britain joined the EEC in 1973 was the abandonment of its Commonwealth partners, who now found their goods and services outside the CET particularly in agricultural products (Burkitt and Baimbridge, 1990).

Whilst Britain can no longer realistically pose as a top power, however, in international diplomacy it still tends to 'punch above its weight', through holding onto its permanent seat on the United Nations Security Council, and maintaining a level of military spending that allows it to join the USA as a junior partner. Hence, Britain's reflex reaction is still to look to its 'special relationship' with the USA, rather than to deeper co-operation in Europe. Moreover, when American and European positions collide, Britain is still usually to be found, isolated amongst its European partners, siding with the USA. However, economically and politically, Britain cannot pretend to be the major player even in Western Europe given that several of the other EU member states are wealthier and it has been long been dominated by a strong Franco-German axis. Consequently, Britain is left trying to come to terms with a future as an island at the extreme north-western edge of an emerging federal European superstate.

The third element is the development of a distinctive legal system, whereby Britain operates a very different legal system from that found on the continent, where the Napoleonic Code forms the basis of law. Consequently, Britain has to make major adjustments compared to other EU nations if, in future, the development of a single European state required close harmonization of national legal systems. For example, the jury system is not generally found in Europe, where magistrates and judges tend to bring in a verdict as well as conducting a trial. Furthermore, the adversarial system of justice is also alien to the European inquisitorial tradition, where an examining magistrate questions witnesses on all sides in an attempt to uncover the truth of a particular case. Finally, continental law also makes much more use of general enabling legislation, that which hands over to the European Commission the right to issue related directives which have the status of new laws and which do not require parliamentary approval. Instead, the British system relies on common law, leaving it to judges to interpret how statutes should apply in particular cases, and binding them to a tradition set by the precedent of earlier rulings.

A further aspect to the contrasting legal systems concerns the different rights of citizenship, such that perhaps the most important difference between the British and continental traditions concerns the different conceptions of citizenship based in the two different legal systems. There is a presumption in continental European law that citizens' rights are granted and safeguarded by the state because it is enshrined in a constitutional document. Legal rights in this tradition are therefore prescriptive. In Britain, by contrast, it has been assumed that individuals have the right to do whatever they choose provided law does not explicitly prohibit it. Legal rights in this tradition are therefore only hampered by proscriptive legislation. This explains why the UK has no equivalent to a Bill of Rights, for in principle we are born with our freedoms and do not look to the state to grant them to us.

A fourth identified difference is that Britain possesses a distinctive type of capitalism typified by the City of London, liberalised markets and its welfare state regime. Hence, whilst the primary emphasis in the move to closer European integration was economic, such that all the EU nations pursue the capitalist market system, British-style capitalism is distinctive compared with that in continental Europe. Hence, with the requirement that twenty-seven European economies should converge, it is the British economy that once again appears most out of step. Hence, through the City of London, the size and significance of its financial services market is a unique feature of the British economy. Not only does London host hundreds of banks, insurance companies and other financial institutions, but its stock exchange and its futures and bonds markets are also the major trading markets in Europe for shares and securities.

However, the City of London is also an indicator of a much more profound underlying difference between the British and continental capitalist systems in terms of the degree of liberalised markets. For example, Albert (1993) contrasts many of the features found in 'Rhine' model countries with those characteristic of the more liberal systems (neo-American model) of capitalism and identifies three key differences in these alternative capitalism systems. Firstly, share capital plays a much more significant role in funding private investment and thereby promoting a short-term perspective in contrast to relying on bank loans to fund new investment. Secondly, the development of a credit culture following the 1980s regulation of financial services that facilitated an increase of credit far greater than anything witnessed in other EU countries. This also contrasts with more of a 'savings culture' in Rhine model countries (excluding private pension funds). Finally, the emergence of a competitive ethos compared to an emphasis on cooperation, based on corporatist structures between government, capital and organised labour. Consequently, such differences form the background to Britain's emphasis to greater supply-side reforms in the European economies through removing subsidies to industry, ending support to agriculture, opening up competition and reducing labour market controls and regulation. However, such reforms are alien on the continent with the Social Chapter, for example, illustrating how Britain is expected to fall into line with the rest of Europe.

Additionally, welfare state regimes further illustrate the divide between the British and continental European capitalist systems. A key study by Esping-Andersen (1990) identified three distinctive 'welfare regimes' in Europe. Firstly, liberal regimes (e.g. Britain) where there is an emphasis on social security as a 'safety net' rather than universal provision. Here the key concern is that welfare provision should not undermine labour market flexibility through an over-generous provision of benefits. Secondly, corporatist welfare regimes (e.g. Germany) where the emphasis is on socially inclusive forms of insurance, but in accordance to people's position in the labour market. Finally, social-democratic welfare regimes (e.g. Scandinavia) where the emphasis is on equality resulting in benefits being both high and universal.

A final general difference between Britain and other EU countries is its distinctively individualistic culture, both traditional and contemporary. Anglo-Saxon individualism has been identified in the pioneering study of Hofstede (1980) relating to how different countries ranked on an individualism/collectivism scale. Within the western group of countries the most individualistic were the USA, Australia, Britain and Canada. In contrast, most EU countries came considerably further down the scale. Such individualism found in contemporary English-speaking cultures, it is argued, can be traced back to the end of feudalism with its restrictions on the sale and purchase of land, which remained in force in parts of continental Europe up to and beyond the time of the French Revolution. Hence, people were used to selling their labour for a wage, and to exchanging goods and services in return for money, such that market-based individualism seems to have predated protestantism and the Reformation by several centuries. It is interesting to note in this regard that it was British thinkers (e.g. John Locke, David Hume, Adam Smith, David Ricardo and John Stuart Mill) who first developed the ideas and principles of liberalism in relation to individual liberty, the free market and the minimal state.

Contemporary individualism can be seen as the pervasive culture that underpins many aspects of British economic and social life in contrast to European norms. Again, privatised provision signals a more individualistic culture illustrated in Britain by a much higher proportion of its population in private or occupational pension schemes, a higher rate of private home ownership and a stronger system of private education. As a corollary, public provision is generally weaker in Britain than elsewhere in Western Europe.

Effects of membership on British politics

A further aspect in which the EU has fundamentally influenced Britain is in relation to its political system regarding its constitution, parliament and elections.

In terms of Britain developing a written constitution by signing the Treaty of Accession in 1972 and subsequent treaties (Maastricht, Amsterdam and Nice etc.) Britain incorporated a lengthy written element in her constitution that takes precedence over 'ordinary' statute law. Consequently, the supremacy of European law is a major limitation on parliament's sovereignty although parliament may at any time repudiate EU membership and the obligations consequent on that membership and leave the EU. Furthermore, EU membership also entailed a significant change to the conduct of elections in Britain. A nationwide referendum was held for the first time in 1975 on Britain's continued membership of the EEC. One unanswered question was what would have happened if parliament had voted one way and the electorate another.

Since 1979 there have been five-yearly elections to the European parliament where the most significant feature of the elections is the derisory turnouts leading to questions of a 'democratic deficit'. This raises problems for the legitimacy of the European project, implying that the enterprise is found largely amongst political elites rather than the broader public. Indeed, identification with and awareness of representative institutions remains much higher at national than European level.

Table 3.2 illustrates the mean turnout statistics over the 1979–2009 period whereby the consequence of compulsory voting is clearly evident albeit essentially now unenforced.[3] There follows a cluster of 10 member states averaging a turnout in excess of 50 per cent, however the majority of countries fall below this key threshold with five below the 30 per cent barrier. Indeed, since the initial elections in 1979 the turnout trend has been inexorably declining, such that the overall EU average figure is now at a precarious 53.4 per cent. Moreover, in relation to the UK, then it is clearly adrift of the other long established, i.e. pre 2004–07 accession countries, ranked in twenty-second place based on average turnout over all European parliamentary elections.

Table 3.2 Summary of European parliament election turnout (1979–2009)(%)

Member state	1979	1984	1989	1994	1999	2004	2009	1979 to 2009*
Belgium**	91.36	92.09	90.73	90.66	91.05	90.81	90.39	91.0
Luxembourg**	88.91	88.79	87.39	88.55	87.27	91.35	90.75	89.0
Malta						82.39	78.79	80.6
Italy	85.65	82.47	81.07	73.6	69.76	71.72	65.05	75.6
Greece**		80.59	80.03	73.18	70.25	63.22	52.61	70.0
Cyprus**						72.5	59.4	66.0
Ireland	63.61	47.56	68.28	43.98	50.21	58.58	58.64	55.8
Germany	65.73	56.76	62.28	60.02	45.19	43	43.3	53.8
EU average turnout	61.99	58.98	58.41	56.67	49.51	45.47	43.0	53.4
Spain			54.71	59.14	63.05	45.14	44.9	53.4
Denmark	47.82	52.38	46.17	52.92	50.46	47.89	59.54	51.0
France	60.71	56.72	48.8	52.71	46.76	42.76	40.63	49.9
Latvia						41.34	53.7	47.5
Austria					49.4	42.43	45.97	45.9
Netherlands	58.12	50.88	47.48	35.69	30.02	39.26	36.75	42.6
Sweden					38.84	37.85	45.53	40.7

Portugal			51.1	35.54	39.93	38.6	36.78	40.4
Bulgaria							38.99	39.0
Hungary						38.5	36.31	37.4
Finland					30.14	39.43	40.3	36.6
Estonia						26.83	43.9	35.4
Lithuania						48.38	20.98	34.7
United Kingdom	32.35	32.57	36.37	36.43	24	38.52	34.7	33.6
Slovenia						28.35	28.33	28.3
Czech Republic						28.3	28.2	28.3
Romania							27.67	27.7
Poland						20.87	24.53	22.7
Slovakia						16.97	19.64	18.3

* = average

** = unenforced compulsory voting

Source: Adapted from Baimbridge (2005)

Both Houses of Parliament have created committees to consider the increasing body of draft European legislation. As more decisions are made in the Council of Ministers by majority voting, so British ministers become less responsible to parliament for Council decisions that they are not able to veto. In terms of administration, Whitehall is becoming more European-minded with civil servants liaising with Brussels to take account of the European dimension of policies, and an increasing number are being seconded to the EU. Ministers are also spending more time negotiating with their ministerial counterparts in the other member states and the views of departments are coordinated through the European Secretariat in the Cabinet Office (Bulmer and Burch 1998). Finally, Britain's judiciary is required under the treaties to give precedence to European law. Not only do British statutes have to be amended to remove any conflict, but also plaintiffs are also able to claim damages against national governments that do not give effect to European laws.

Table 3.3 Summary of policy competences

Policy competence (predominantly located in the EU)	Policy competence (a combination of EU and national governments)	Policy competence (predominantly located in national governments or through intergovernmental agreement)

Agriculture	Environmental	Foreign affairs
Trade	Transport	Macro-economic policy
Fishing	Social policy	Health
Competition	Regional policy	Education
Consumer protection	Research and technology	Defence
Monetary policy (EMU)		Drugs
		Welfare benefits
		Law and order

Source: Richards and Smith (2002)

Evidently, a consequence of EU membership has been that the state has lost a significant degree of autonomy in a whole range of policy areas; these are summarised in Table 3.3 which illustrates how most policy areas now possess an EU element and, in particular, a significant number are either wholly or partially devolved from national governments. Thus, despite the argument that parliamentary sovereignty is retained because the UK has the right to leave the EU if it so chooses, the reality is that the role of parliament is often to merely ratify decisions made in the EU. Consequently, the EU appears to undermine the territorial integrity of its member states as decisions made outside the nation state at the European level are being implemented within Britain. These factors suggest that the autonomy of the British state is now greatly restricted by EU membership, and that policy-making has increasingly become a partnership between the British government, other member states, and the institutions of the EU. Indeed, the scope and depth of policy-making at the EU-level have dramatically increased as it has completed the internal market and absorbed the institutional reforms of the Single European Act (1986), which established qualified majority voting in the Council of Ministers and increased the power of the European parliament. The TEU and Lisbon (Reform) Treaty further expanded EU competencies and the scope of qualified majority voting together with providing the European Parliament with a veto on certain types of legislation. The way the EU is designed, the difficulty of controlling the Commission, the problems with agreeing to restrain the process of integration, the unique informational base of the Commission, the regulatory powers of the Commission and the European Court of Justice, and the unintended consequences of institutional change all make it difficult for national governments to control the EU.

Conclusion

Although European leaders have always made clear their view that the European project recognizes and even celebrates cultural diversity, the European project is built on a continental cultural heritage which is contrary to Britain's historical links to North America and its former empire, reinforced by a common language, its individualistic culture and its system of law. However, of particular importance for this book is the fundamental difference in economic structures. Britain's economy depends to a much greater extent on its financial sector; it has a much smaller and more capital-intensive agricultural sector; it still trades significantly with non-EU countries; and its liberal competitive instincts align it much more closely with the United States than with the corporatist traditions of Western Europe.

In summary, as the EU moves closer to complete political and monetary union, it is Britain that continues to make the most adjustments. In particular, British law is out of step with the emerging system of European law and the British economy is out of step with European regulated labour markets and corporatist management structures. Given this record of difficult adjustment to European integration it is understandable if there is an increasing desire for Britain to slow down, pause, or even rethink the whole EU project.

Notes

[1] Except, *inter alia,* in the area of tax harmonisation that still relies on unanimity.

[2] Despite the formulation of a common foreign and security policy, the experience has, at best, been mixed with failure to forge a coherent policy towards the Balkans, whilst there were well-publicised splits over Iraq.

[3] For the calculation of EP election turnout the initial 'out of sequence' EP elections of accession countries (Spain, Portugal, Sweden, Austria and Finland) are counted as per the immediately prior EP election, otherwise these results would be omitted from the quinquennial calculations. Moreover, the unweighted member state turnout is used in all tables and calculations.

CHAPTER 4

CONSEQUENCES OF EU MEMBERSHIP

Introduction

The UK's relationship with the EU has been controversial ever since the Treaty of Rome established the latter. Indeed, public opinion polls since the early 1990s demonstrate a majority opinion amongst the UK electorate that remains critical of the EU, with a not insignificant number desiring withdrawal. In the face of such apparent hostility towards further economic and political integration, the British establishment has remained remarkably united, not only in supporting continued membership of the EU, but in fostering wider and deeper economic integration. Successive governments claimed that the benefits of EU membership are 'self-evident' (e.g. Lord Hanley, 3 July 1995, House of Lords), so that the UK must remain at the heart of Europe; otherwise it would lose crucial political influence and millions of jobs. Moreover, when the previous Labour government was committed to holding a referendum relating to potential EMU membership, it assiduously avoided undertaking the kind of information distribution and political campaign that is required if informed decisions are to be taken by British citizens. Furthermore, the claim is repeatedly made that even a slight weakening in the trend towards greater unification would cost the UK jobs and influence, never mind what would occur if the UK voted to withdraw from EU membership. Yet, governments of all colours have been remarkably reticent to undertake an independent cost-benefit analysis of UK membership.

The reason for this apparent conundrum is that at least in purely economic terms, it is doubtful that the UK has received a net benefit from EU membership. Indeed, even when taking political considerations into account, former Chancellor of the Exchequer, Norman Lamont argued that: 'The advantages of the European Union are remarkably elusive ... I cannot pinpoint a single concrete economic advantage that unambiguously comes to this country because of our membership.'

This chapter therefore seeks to test Lamont's claim by compensating for the absence of an official cost-benefit analysis and reviewing the evidence relating to the historical advantages and disadvantages arising from EU membership for the British economy in relation to both economic-related matters and EU institutional arrangements.

The balance of trade

After the UK's accession, tariffs on trade in manufactures between Britain and EU member countries were eliminated in five equal steps of 20 per cent implemented on 1 April 1973, 1 January 1974, 1 January 1975, 1 January 1976 and 1 July 1977. UK quantitative restrictions on EU trade were abolished on 1 January 1973, except for a few based on non-economic grounds, such as public morality and security. The UK was compelled to apply the Common External Tariff (CET) to imports from all countries not belonging to, or enjoying special arrangements with, the EU. The CET was applied in four stages of 40 per cent on 1 January 1974, 20 per cent on 1 January 1975, 20 per cent on 1 January 1976 and 20 per cent on 1 July 1977.

When Britain joined the EU, it was accepted that entry would impose a balance of payments cost in the form of contributions to the EU budget and higher prices for imported food. These effects indeed occurred, but were intensified by a sharp deterioration in the UK balance of trade with the EU. It fell from a surplus of £385 million in 1970 (effectively the last pre-entry year) to a deficit of £12.6 billion by 1988. According to the governments' own figures, published in the annual Balance of Payments Accounts, the UK suffered a total accumulated trading deficit of £90.6 billion with the EU during the 27 years to 2000. Over the same period, the UK enjoyed a trading surplus of £70.9 billion with the rest of the world. In fact, the deficit is larger than official statistics suggest. First, they are a summation of historical statistics, not adjusted for inflation. Second they take no account of the Antwerp–Rotterdam effect, which incorrectly allocates approximately 10 per cent of British exports to the EU rather than to the rest of the world, because they go initially to the continent for containerisation before being dispatched internationally.

Such a substantial volume of resources, drained from the British economy, has led to deflationary budgetary and monetary policies to restore balance of trade equilibrium by lowering relative production costs. However, output and employment simultaneously fall, which in turn generates less favourable investment prospects. The resulting loss of efficiency further worsens the balance of trade, which necessitates more deflationary policies, causing lower growth. It is difficult for this spiral of relative decline to be reversed whilst the UK remains subject to a very large trade deficit with other EU member states. Orthodox policies to reduce trade deficits involve the deflation of the economy, thereby relying upon rising unemployment to choke off demand for imported goods. Unfortunately, this will leave the UK economy growing more slowly, and carrying higher rates of unemployment, than would otherwise have occurred, thus contradicting the economic advantages that were advocated in the 1970s relating to the trade benefits of EU membership.

A second argument used to justify UK membership of the EU claims that this is the source of a majority of UK trade and therefore withdrawal from the EU trade bloc, or even refusal to participate in the eurozone, would have disastrous consequences for UK exports and hence employment prospects. Unfortunately, this claim is based upon a misleading premise if statistics are used selectively, whereby trade is restricted to goods and services, and the remainder of the current account (i.e. investment income and transfers) is discounted. However, a detailed analysis reveals that approximately only 48 per cent of the UK's current account relates to the EU, and 43 per cent occurs with euro participants. Indeed, just as much trade takes place with the USA as France and Germany combined. Thus, although the UK is deeply involved in trading to EU member states, it remains a minority of total trade. Moreover, the EU trade remains in significant deficit, whereas non-EU trade generates a surplus, signifying that a reallocation of trade-creating resources to non-EU areas may contribute towards reducing the UK's overall trade deficit.

Furthermore, the significance of the US dollar is an additional factor impacting upon the importance of the EU for UK trade. Many commodities (including oil, gas, information technology, pharmaceuticals and high-technology electronic equipment) are priced and exchanged in dollars. Even within the eurozone, as much UK trade (around 25 per cent) occurs in dollars as in the eurozone currencies. Furthermore, these statistics relate to goods only, so that they inevitably overstate the role of the euro. Given the greater importance of the dollar than the euro to UK trade, and noting that over the last decade the pound–dollar relationship has proved to be the most stable currency exchange rate in the world, it is clear that joining the euro will increase volatility in the UK's trade and investment.

Additionally, in the long term, the share of British trade with the current members of the eurozone is likely to decline. The population of the eurozone is projected by the US Census Bureau to fall by over 7 per cent to 2050, whilst the population of most of the rest of the world is still rising. In some parts of Asia and the Middle East annual population expansion is predicted to be as high as 3 per cent. Assuming that per capita growth rates are the same across EU and non-EU countries, the EU's share of the British current account will fall to less than 40 per cent by 2050. If the non-EU nations enjoy higher per capita growth, which is probable on recent trends, then the EU's share will decline below 30 per cent. Although the eurozone will remain a significant trading bloc, future world changes in population and income levels will erode its importance. It is therefore ironic that, as the UK ponders abandoning the pound for the euro, the importance of the eurozone is declining.

The Common Agricultural Policy

Since the abolition of the Corn Laws in 1846, Britain's policy was to allow free entry to the lowest cost foodstuffs, which benefited industry because workers obtained their food at prices competitive with our rivals in manufacturing. Additionally the British public possessed more income to spend on other goods, whilst the countries from which the UK imported food spent on commodities produced in Britain. This beneficial cumulative process was destroyed by the UK's accession to the EU.

The desire of France and Germany to protect farmers from external competition, coupled with the French intention to secure outlets for the products of their former colonies, initially held the EU together. The French in particular were determined that the UK should never be allowed to join unless it abandoned its cheap food programme. Indeed, a Common Agricultural Policy (CAP) was incorporated within the EU integration strategy to maintain the balance of interests between its original six members. This is operated by EU officials, who fix a common minimum price for given foods whatever the world level of prices for agricultural commodities, by manipulating the quantity to which consumers enjoy access.

Consequently, in the context of the ongoing free market orientated developments in the EU, it seems rather perverse that agriculture should continue to be treated so differently. It is somewhat ironic that whilst the CAP is seen as a cornerstone of European integration, it is a policy where competing national interests have been longstanding.

This has been seen in two ways: first, in how the Council of Ministers has fought to retain power from supranational institutions such as the European parliament and second, in how the member states have lined up against each other in the battles over reform as was highlighted by the confrontation between Britain and France in June 2005. This contrast remains evident when examining the experience of the last decade, where on the one hand significant progress has been made in advancing the principles of competition and barrier-free trade under the auspices of the single market, whilst Europeans continue to spend just under half of the EU's budgetary resources subsidising a farming sector which today accounts for merely two per cent of EU(15) GDP. Justifiably, greater support for agriculture was taken from the political standpoint of ensuring food security and continued political stability in the early post-war years, whilst securing a fair standard of living for the rural community (Baimbridge *et al.*, 2004).

A number of potential contradictions were also observed. There is evidence that farmers have had little influence over the shaping of recent CAP reforms. Moreover, ministers of agriculture have been joined, even supplanted, by ministers of finance in negotiating these reforms. Yet, despite this evidence that national agricultural policy communities have been weakening, the level of spending on the CAP has been sustained. Typically, those who block reform are receiving large CAP transfers, together with experiencing reduced variability in their share of CAP spending. Those seeking CAP reform are not always major net contributors to CAP spending, but they are most likely to be net contributors to the EU budget overall. Indeed, as outlined above, given the dominance of CAP spending in the EU budget negotiations over the CAP and its spending have transcended the agricultural arena. Therefore, it is suggested that decision makers might still seek to defend the pattern of transfers established at the outset of the CAP (Ackrill, 2005).

The constraints imposed by the CAP raised the British cost of living, whilst encouraging an inefficient transfer of resources into agricultural output away from more productive manufacturing and services. Moreover, because the UK has traditionally been a net importer of foodstuffs, higher food prices represented deterioration in the UK's terms of trade, whilst the inflationary impact upon UK exports damaged the balance of payments (Burkitt *et al.*, 1992, 1996). A return to the deficiency payments system that operated in Britain from 1947 to 1973 is the most efficient alternative. The saving upon food expenditure and taxation, combined with the availability of cheaper food, would be counter-inflationary, as it lowers the retail price index and increases demand, thus reducing unit costs. Moreover, lower food prices lead to smaller pay increases, so cutting labour costs throughout the economy, whilst the transfer of income from the poor to the rich, through higher food prices, would end. Additionally, one solution to the recent crisis in British agriculture is to embrace organic, environmentally sustainable land management and farming techniques. However, it is a solution that the CAP precludes.

Additionally, the financial discipline element of the 2003 reform will, however, provide a serious challenge to the budgetary status quo when it becomes operational in 2007, because it presents the very real possibility of member states having to choose either to make cuts to direct payments or allow a spending limit to be breached. However, the shift in Europe toward capital-intensive technology-based industries moves hand in hand with World Trade Organisation (WTO) agreements designed to erode protectionist world agricultural markets and aid the development of poorer countries in an earlier stage of their development cycle. This change in doctrine from mercantilism to globalisation leaves European agriculture in a very different position to that of 50 years ago, whilst changes in consumer expectations of agriculture in the twenty-first century have catalysed the beginnings of a reorientation in EU agricultural policy (Baimbridge *et al.*, 2004).

The Common Fisheries Policy

The Common Fisheries Policy (CFP) constitutes a prime example of how the UK gave away control of its resources due to EU accession. Immediately prior to Britain's entry, the six original members, without sanction from the Treaty of Rome, devised the CFP as a way of gaining access to the 60–80 per cent of fish in EU waters, which lay within the British Territorial Limit. In his eagerness to join the EU, Edward Heath agreed to this self-interested manoeuvre, accepting fish to be 'a common European resource' which any member could catch anywhere in the Community. Through such acceptance, he gave away part of UK citizens' birthright and sowed the seeds for the decline of the UK fishing industry.

Whilst the number of fish consumed in 1988 was approximately equal to the 1997 level, the proportion provided by UK vessels had fallen from over 85 per cent to only 61 per cent, with imports rising threefold. When transitory agreements expired, the UK had to negotiate hard to prevent more than 40 Spanish boats from fishing in the 100,000 mile 'Irish Box' at any one time. Spain possesses the world's largest fishing fleet, with a tonnage of 587,173 in 1997, but enjoys relatively few domestic waters, so that it sought to take advantage of the CFP to fish intensively in British waters.

Over-fishing is the consequence of limited stocks supporting an influx of new fleets, embodying improved technology, which enables larger catches. In 1972 some 300,000 tonnes of cod were taken from the North Sea, but in 1999 fisherman only managed to catch 60 per cent of the total EU quota of 81,000 tonnes. The EU response to this plundering of a scarce natural resource was not to re-establish national fishing rights, but to impose a system of quotas, or 'total allowable catches', to restrict the number of fish landed in a year. As each fishing vessel receives its share of the quota, the right for non-UK vessels to fish in UK territorial waters is enshrined. However, quotas only relate to the landing of certain categories of fish. The EU has made no cut in industrial quotas, so allowing the Danish fleet to continue removing vast quantities of the small fish on which larger species, such as cod and haddock, depend for food.

Unless drastic action is taken to stop over-fishing there will be no more cod, haddock, or monkfish left anywhere from the North Sea to the Irish Box. The EU administered its quotas with such corruption, cynicism and incompetence that barely an edible fish remains within its jurisdiction. In contrast, Iceland, having won the Cod War in the 1970s, took its scientists' predictions seriously and introduced measures that ensure it still enjoys a sustainable supply of fish. The EU could, if it wanted, close down fisheries temporarily and compensate (or retrain) fishermen until stocks recover. Apart from a token reduction in fish quotas (which are bound to be broken because they are never enforced), the EU has decided that the short-term need of vested interests are more important than the long-term survival of an industry and a whole ecosystem.

The Save Britain's Fish Campaign argues that the quota failure should be replaced by a conservation strategy, based upon the utilisation of new technology which can control the size and species of fish caught in trawler nets. This technology is deployed by the Canadian and Norwegian governments, but is rejected by the EU. In view of the CFP's failings, the reluctance of the EU to reform and the urgency of minimising further losses of fish stocks, it appears inevitable that the UK should withdraw from the CFP if it is to protect its few remaining fisheries effectively.

The Royal Society of Edinburgh (2004) forwarded three major recommendations regarding the impact of the CFP. Firstly, that the existing 12 mile limits be made permanent instead of being subject to renewal every 10 years. Secondly, it recommended that arrangements for use of EU Structural Funds in order to make maximum use of the Financial Instruments for Fisheries Guidance and other Funds for the economic diversification of fisheries-dependent areas are reviewed. Thirdly, the position of the EU's exclusive competence for conservation of marine biological resources should be reconsidered, with a view to having this deleted from the proposed EU Constitution so that the principle of subsidiarity applies to fisheries, as it does to other matters.

In summary, the CFP has been an unmitigated disaster for UK fishermen, and UK consumers who faced price rises due to restricted supply and lower utilisation of vessel capacity. In 1973 between 60–80 per cent of fish within EU waters lay within the British Territorial Limit, yet by 1996 the UK's share of catches within the EU was only 12.7 per cent. A year later, the UK's share of catches within the EU's fishing tonnage was a mere 12.3 per cent (Eurostat Yearbook, 1998–9). These statistics provide a crippling indictment of the CFP's impact upon the UK fishing industry. The conclusion is inescapable; Britain's fishermen are being betrayed in the pursuit of EU integration by those elected to defend them.

Single internal market

Since the inception of the first treaty over 50 years ago, the principle of a borderless zone for the trade of goods and services and free movement of factors of production has remained at the heart of European thinking. The Single European Act (SEA), which was adopted by the UK parliament in 1986 and became European Law in 1987, was intended to create a single, unified internal market covering all member states by 31 December 1992. By this date, all formal trade barriers had to be removed, including border controls, whilst ensuring the free movement of capital, people, goods and services between members. The Single Internal Market (SIM) program was a watershed in the EU's development, and although seen at the time as revolutionary, it was really part of an evolutionary process. Now just over 15 years after the 1992 program, it is clear that great strides have been made, although the actual benefits are still less than those projected.

The economic rationale was presented in a report prepared for the EU Commission (Cecchini, 1988), which claimed that consumers would be able to buy cheaper goods after the removal of non-tariff barriers due to increased competition between firms and greater exploitation of economies of scale made possible by a larger market place. The report suggested these benefits would increase EU GDP by 7 per cent and create five million new jobs across the Union. This prediction, however, assumed that the potential for greater economies of scale actually existed, and that a single market will not lead to increased monopolisation and consequent retention of monopoly profits. Since non-tariff barriers did not present large obstacles to trade amongst the EU nations before the single internal market (SIM), it was unlikely that their removal would lead to significant economies of scale being achieved, which had not already been attained.

In addition, a substantial part of Cecchini's estimated benefits were supposed to come from supply-side effects that reduced inflation and balance of payments constraints. Thus greater economic activity would provide increased resources for reflationary government expenditure. To the extent that the loosening of restraints on growth depend upon increasing competition and utilising economies of scale, if these advantages fail to materialise then eventual supply-side benefits will be lower than predicted. Furthermore, Cecchini's assumption of concerted reflation amongst EU nations was always implausible and was superseded by deflationary imperatives demanded by ERM membership and the Maastricht Treaty's fiscal convergence criteria that all members are committed to achieving. Consequently, without co-ordinated reflation, a considerable proportion of Cecchini's predicted benefits flowing from the SEA would not materialise (Burkitt and Baimbridge, 1990, 1991). Additionally, some aspects were given too much significance such as economies of scale, whilst others such as FDI have risen far than expected (Harrop, 2005).

The SIM is frequently cited as the prime economic reason for the UK's participation in the EU. In particular, for Britain's political and business establishment, the belief that it generates enormous benefits has become an unqualified article of faith. However, how accurate is this assessment?

In the relatively protectionist world of the 1960s and 1970s, significant potential benefits could accrue from EU membership, due to the absence of previously high tariffs *within* the single market. Whilst the successive rounds of GATT reduced average tariffs on manufactured goods from their immediate post-1945 levels of over 40 per cent, they remained above 20 per cent. The attraction of free trade within the EU, whose member economies grew above the industrial average before 1973 (but failed to do so subsequently), appeared considerable despite the economic and political burdens imposed by accession. However, successive waves of trade liberalisation suggest that the UK would not join the EU for trade reasons today. The Uruguay Round (1986–94) of world trade negotiations reduced the average tariff on trade manufactures between developed countries to a mere 3.8 per cent, scarcely a barrier for any exporters enjoying sizeable profit margins. Consequently, in the twenty-first century, the developed world is closer to free trade than it has ever been.

Experience to date provides no support for the established belief that the SIM provides significant benefits for the UK (Stewart-Brown, 1999a, 1999b). With the significant exception of Japanese car producers (who account for only 1.5 per cent of foreign direct investment into Britain), manufacturers enjoy access to the SIM, wherever they are located. The weight of evidence is clear; the assumption of the British governing class, articulated by Charles Kennedy in *The Times* on 26 September 1999 that 'Britain gains so much from membership of the European Union, it is hard to believe that anyone can still question that it is in our national interest', lacks any empirical basis in the contemporary, low tariff world. Instead, indications suggest that the SIM has widened, not diminish, the UK's trade deficit with other EU nations.

In the absence of the reflationary policies assumed by Cecchini (1988), which are essentially Keynesian measures which could be implemented without the SEA, the final effect on UK growth and employment rates is at best marginal, and at worst will further damage the UK economy at a time when the dynamics of EU membership are increasingly adverse.

Undoubtedly, remarkable progress has been made in terms of EU policy to forge ahead with the creation of a truly integrated market system. However, national government expenditure still generates a small proportion of cross-border trade, whilst external trade policy is not yet completely harmonised. Furthermore, discrepancies remain in the tax system across member states and the notion of free labour mobility, whilst true in theory, is minimal in practise. Indeed, it is a mistake to take the SIM for granted, and in May 2003 the Commission published its SIM strategy until 2006 in response to a Commission report that listed 92 barriers encountered by business, and proposed a ten-point plan to improve the situation (Harrop, 2005). These apparent deficiencies are widely recognised as being attributed to the absence of a supra-national EU government and associated budget mechanism. Moreover, the common usage of multiple spoken languages and rich diversity of traditions and customs are certainly admirable pan-European features, but seriously inhibit intra-EU labour migration (Baimbridge *et al.*, 2004).

The EU budget

European finances are much more complicated than the mere size of the budget suggests. Whilst the revenue side restricts the size of the budget due to the balanced budget requirement and the system of own resources that is largely based on member states' contributions, the EU determines the structure of spending. Compulsory spending (agricultural expenditure) is strongly influenced by the Council and the Commission, and non-compulsory spending (structural funds) is mainly determined by the parliament (Feld, 2005).

The EU budget is financed through four mechanisms: agricultural levies, customs duties, a proportion of VAT receipts based on a nationally harmonised basket of goods and services, and a calculation based upon the size of each member's GDP. However, as recently as 1990 VAT receipts made the largest contribution although these are biased against members like the UK whose historically higher-than-average consumption rates caused overpayment to the EU in comparison to the GDP per capita calculation. Furthermore the EU ignores VAT exemptions that require member states to transfer the same amount of revenue to the EU budget whether or not the commodities paid full rates of VAT. This method of funding was neither fair nor transparent, so that the EU eventually restructured its revenue collection by ensuring that the fourth resource based upon national wealth is the principal contributor to financing the budget.

However, the pattern of EU expenditure and the sources of its revenue are structured so that the UK consistently contributes a greater proportion of EU finances than it receives in return or than is warranted by its national income relative to that of other member states. This phenomenon did not arise by accident, but from the inherent structure of the EU budget and will persist in the future. Indeed, whilst the accession of Austria, Finland and Sweden partially facilitated the expansion of revenues because all three countries were richer than the EU average, this has been superseded by the recent Central and Eastern enlargement through admitting member states whose GDP per capita is typically less than half the EU average, which possesses consequences for regional and agricultural policy. This presents a fundamental challenge to EU policy makers, largely because it involves the costly supra-national policies of structural funding and the CAP (Baimbridge *et al.*, 2004). Consequently, existing net contributors have been forced to increase payments to the EU budget, with the UK's net contribution more than doubling.

An examination of the EU budget reveals that approximately 45 per cent of the own resources are used to finance the CAP, whilst another

30 per cent are allocated toward structural policies including social, regional and rural development. Thus, approximately 75 per cent of the budget is allocated on either protecting one sector from global competition or to reduce economic disparities that exist between the EU's richest and poorest members (Baimbridge *et al.*, 2004). Hence, reform of the EU budget is long overdue, for it still requires the UK to pay for the storage of unsold, over-priced agricultural products, which East European outlets could supply at a lower cost simultaneously contributing towards these countries' economic regeneration.

Finally, when analysing the structure of revenue and spending, the question emerges of why a European budget is actually needed? Theoretical guidelines, such as those from the economic theory of federalism, suggest that aside from the provision of the internal market, EU-wide public goods, or a need for coordination at the EU level, may exist. The European Convention suggests further attempts to coordinate these policies, but is far from proposing any dominant competence of the Union. It does not propose far-reaching additional spending competencies of the EU, nor does it say much about additional own resources or coordination of taxation. Rather it only suggests abolishing the distinction between compulsory and non-compulsory spending, and increasing coordination among member states in cases of tax fraud. Enlargement is also not expected to greatly affect spending or revenue. However, the current tax reforms in Eastern European countries indicate that tax competition in the enlarged Europe will be even more intense than today. It remains to be seen whether this will finally lead to additional restrictions of national sovereignty in taxation (Feld, 2005).

The cost of ERM membership

The European Monetary System (EMS) was created after the break up of the Bretton Woods fixed exchange rate system, with the Exchange Rate Mechanism (ERM) established in 1979. Within a fixed exchange rate mechanism, when a currency falls to its permitted minimum, the government is forced to change economic policy to avoid breaking the imposed band. Such a strategy can take the form of using official reserves to purchase one's own currency (if too low in value) or purchase other currencies (if too high). The ERM was designed to provide exchange rate stability through mutual cooperation between participating countries' central banks to safeguard their currencies against short-term speculation, whilst removing uncertainty from trade. Exchange rate movements within the permitted band ensured that a currency did not become fundamentally misaligned, with devastating consequences for employment and output.

However, in the run-up to establishing the single currency, the ERM underwent a significant evolution. Individual currencies were no longer protected by exchange controls, but realignments were all but forbidden on the ground that a nation should demonstrate the stability of its currency with other participants prior to EMU entry. At this point the UK decided to become a member of the ERM in October 1990, at a fixed central parity of 2.95 Deutschmarks to the pound, a rate intended to put pressure upon the UK economy to reduce inflation rather than setting a competitive exchange rate. Unsurprisingly, this chosen rate, and ERM membership itself, proved to be a mistake.

The period of ERM membership, from October 1990 to September 1992, was a disaster for the British economy. The restraints imposed upon productive activity due to an over-valued currency were so severe that the economy headed into recession. During the two years of membership, GDP shrunk by 3.8 per cent, being associated with six out of eight quarters of negative growth. Under these circumstances, unemployment rose by 1.2 million to a total of 2.85 million on official government figures.

Whilst it would be exaggerated to claim that this period of economic decline was caused solely by ERM membership, it is worth noting that the economy expanded by an average of 2 per cent per annum immediately prior to membership and also in its aftermath. Moreover, the unemployment rate was 5.5 per cent before sterling joined the ERM, rose sharply afterwards, but started to fall again once the UK departed. Of course, other factors influenced these developments (e.g. German reunification), but it was the restrictions imposed upon macroeconomic policy by the ERM, which prevented the UK from responding to deflationary pressures by expansionary fiscal and monetary policy to limit the damage inflicted upon jobs and output.

In seeking to measure the extent to which ERM membership damaged the UK economy, our first calculation focuses upon the rise in unemployment. The UK Treasury believes that the average unemployed person costs the state £9,000 a year in terms of benefits paid and taxes foregone. Combining that figure with the 1.2 million increase in unemployment during the UK's two year membership of the ERM the cost to the Treasury can be estimated at £10.8 billion, equivalent to 1.8 per cent of the then UK GDP.

A second element refers to the potential increase in output and living standards that were foregone during these two years. It includes not only the 3.9 per cent absolute decline in GDP during ERM membership, which amounts to £23.1 billion at 1992 prices, but additionally incorporates an estimate of the growth that the economy would achieve in a normal year. The long-term trend of the UK economy is estimated to be approximately 2.5 per cent per annum, so that any deviation from this trend must be taken into account. Without ERM membership, UK GDP would have been expected to be around 5.0 per cent higher (i.e. two years' expansion at 2.5 per cent a year), whilst during those two years it fell by 3.9 per cent. When these two statistics are added together, the cost of lost output lies in the region of £53.4 billion in 1992 prices (i.e. approximately 9 per cent of national income).

Third, to the unemployment and output costs must be added the price of defending sterling within its ERM parity. Although ultimately unsuccessful, the UK government spent an estimated £15 million of its foreign reserves, trying to resist the speculative attack that ended ERM membership. After Britain left the ERM and sterling devalued by 20 per cent and the Bank of England sought to rebuild its foreign exchange holdings, but discovered that each pound now bought 20 per cent less than previously. Therefore, the £15 billion reserves were devaluated by a fifth, costing Britain an additional £3 billion.

In summary, adding the costs borne by the UK Treasury (£10.8 billion), lost output (£53.4 billion) and the fall in value of the UK's official reserves (£3 billion), the ERM experiment cost £67.2 billion or 11.3 per cent of 1992 UK GDP. Such sums illustrate the price exacted by fixed exchange rate mechanisms, an ominous indication of the burden imposed on those countries operating the single currency.

The single currency

One of the greatest milestones of political and economic integration has been the creation of the single European currency, the scale and scope of its theoretical and applied economic connotations we have critically evaluated elsewhere (Baimbridge *et al.*, 2000, 2004, 2006; Baimbridge and Whyman, 2008). Hence, in summary the ethos of this initiative was the need to increase transparency between member states' trade by eliminating transactions costs arising from the usage of national currencies. In eliminating such costs, price transparency between member states would enhance competitive forces, and also reduce risk associated with cross border investments. Furthermore, in clearing a path for Monetary Union under the auspices of the Treaty on European Union (TEU), qualification standards on economic convergence targets for inflation, budgetary discipline and interest rates had a beneficial effect on those countries which had up until that time been rather lax with their fiscal and monetary discipline (Baimbridge *et al.*, 2004).

Clearly this undertaking has not been without risks either, particularly given the absence of any EU government or budget mechanism to preside over the system. Furthermore, the removal of national central banks from signatory members and the introduction of rules governing both budgetary and public debt limits under the auspices of the Stability and Growth Pact (SGP) opened up potentially dangerous consequences to member states that fall out of synchronisation with the European business cycle. Indeed, without traditional means of macroeconomic management, many argue that the success of the currency for members in the long term relies at least partly on advances in improving labour market flexibility both within and between member states. The importance of economic alignment within the common currency scheme has, to some extent, been highlighted by current events whereby it is unfortunate for the architects of the SGP that the two largest economies within the eurozone, France and Germany, have breached this fiscal condition citing the need to stimulate sluggish economic growth. This is unlikely to bode well with smaller members in the eurozone who have adhered to the guidelines, as it does not appear that any form of discipline under the auspices of the SGP agreement will be administered (Baimbridge *et al.*, 2004). In light of these challenges, it may be that flanking policies and the role of new institutions (such as the Eurogroup) might have to be reconsidered as new countries join EMU. Furthermore, although not immediately likely, it is not unthinkable, that countries will leave the eurozone (Verdun, 2005). This final series of dilemmas regarding the sustainability of the eurozone has recently taken on greater significance following the repercussions of the 2008 credit crunch recession, which has revealed the fundamental flaws inherent within the EMU architecture. Consequently, we discuss these and potential solutions in greater depth in Chapter 5.

Conclusion

The UK's membership in the EU to date has proved to be rather disappointing to those early pioneers of European integration via the balance of trade, the CAP, the CFP, the EU budget the ERM and the potential of the single currency. Moreover, such costs are not simply a one-off payment borne in the past; the majority exert an annual burden that will continue indefinitely and may even intensify over time. For example, the EU Commission has frequently raised the possibility of eliminating the UK's budget rebate, a change which would substantially increase the net cost of EU membership, whilst agricultural protectionism, even after repeated reform attempts, will remain costly to the UK economy and consumer for the foreseeable future. Moreover, the devastating experience of ERM participation casts considerable doubt upon EMU membership since a forced exit from this scheme would bear a considerably greater cost. Indeed, even the SIM, the one area where most commentators would have assumed the UK to be a net beneficiary of European integration, produces conflicting evidence, suggesting the necessity for cautious analysis simply to determine whether or not the extension of free trade between EU member states has in fact been beneficial for the UK economy.

Additionally, this chapter has highlighted future, potentially problematic, issues for Britain given the overall development of the EU in these key areas. However, such is the scope of the modern EU that a single chapter cannot seek to encompass the myriad of topics associated with it (e.g. European Council and the Council of the European Union; the European Commission; the European Parliament; judicial, controlling, and advisory institutions; the EU budget; Single Internal Market; the Common Foreign and Security Policy; the Common Agricultural Policy; energy policy; environmental policy; transport policy; regional policy; social policy; development policy; enlargement; Economic and Monetary Union; the European Central Bank.), all of which are likely to significantly impinge upon the UK's ability for democratic self-governance.

CHAPTER 5

THE EURO AS A FLAWED CURRENCY AREA

Introduction

Historically the most obvious areas where EU membership has imposed significant net costs upon the UK economy relate, firstly, to the net UK contribution to the EU budget of over £50 billion. Secondly, agricultural protectionism through the Common Agricultural Policy (CAP) has caused food prices to remain 7 per cent above world prices, costing an average British family £36 per week (Burkitt *et al.*, 1996). Black (2000) argues that unilateral withdrawal from the CAP alone would result in significant budgetary savings, where the loss in revenues to farmers would be more than compensated by significant welfare gains to consumers from cheaper food prices arising from trade diversion and creation effects. Similarly, Pain and Young (2004) suggest that UK food prices could be reduced by as much as 20 per cent on leaving the EU. This assertion is also supported by Hindley and Howe (1996), Leach (2000), Milne (2004) and Minford *et al.* (2005:6) who predict a UK net cost ranging from 1–1.5 per cent of GDP, some £10-15 billion, from EU membership largely due to the CAP. Thirdly, Deva (2002) calculates that approximately 40 per cent of all legislation that affects Britain arises from the EU, whereby the costs of regulation and harmonisation of goods and services will have a significant net cost for companies and organisations operating within the UK. Thus, in terms of UK GDP, regulation is estimated to cost between 2 per cent (Milne, 2004) and 6 per cent (Minford *et al.*, 2005). Finally, EU experimentation with fixed exchange rates has proven to be disastrous for the UK economy, with its 1990–92 ERM membership resulting in GDP shrinking by 3.8 per cent, unemployment rising by 1.2 million thereby cumulatively costing the UK economy over £67 billion or 11.3 per cent of 1992 UK GDP in terms of lost potential output (Burkitt *et al.*, 1996). There is little reason to assume that membership of EMU would prove any more fruitful in terms of the operation of the European Central Bank, together with the tight fiscal rules established in the Stability and Growth Pact, which have contributed to the eurozone economy suffering a decade or more of slow growth (Baimbridge, 2006; Michie, 2006; Ormerod, 2006; Sawyer and Arestis, 2006; Whyman *et al.*, 2006).

In relation to trade, the one area where many authors tend to find strong benefits for continued UK membership of the EU, the data is more complex. For example, whilst the EU does represent approximately 48 per cent of UK trade (and the eurozone 43 per cent), more exports are priced in terms of dollars (i.e. oil and gas, aerospace, pharmaceuticals) than in euros. Furthermore, it is the net balance of trade that is important for the prosperity and future development potential of the UK economy, not the absolute amount of trade taking place. Thus commentators frequently include erroneous measures such as emigration and the number of holidays that UK citizens take abroad in warmer countries as evidence of a 'profound europeanisation' of the UK economy (Aspinwall, 2003). Far more significantly, the UK has suffered a total accumulated trading deficit of over £90 billion with the EU, whereas during the same period it has enjoyed a trading surplus of over £70 billion with the rest of the world. Such a substantial volume of resources, drained from the British economy, will have contributed to lower economic growth, leading to fewer jobs in the UK (particularly in manufacturing industry) than would otherwise have been the case (Baimbridge and Whyman, 2008). Moreover, the substantial expansion in European growth rates that the EU's *Cecchini Report* (Cecchini, 1988) predicted would result from the creation of the Single Internal Market (SIM) have not materialised as predicted (Burkitt and Baimbridge, 1990, 1991). Consequently, Milne (2004) and Minford *et al.* (2005) estimate a net cost for the UK economy, arising from trade-related matters, varying between 0.1 per cent and 2.5 per cent of UK GDP.

However, the above costs relating to EU membership potentially pale into relative insignificance compared to those associated with the collapse of the European single currency. Indeed, since the inception of the euro many commentators have agued that, despite its resilience to immediate collapse due to the volume of political and, from 2010, financial capital invested in it by the European Union establishment, it remains a fundamentally flawed creation (Baimbridge *et al.*, 1999; Minford, 2002; Milne, 2004; Baimbridge and Whyman, 2008). The reasons are varied: the eurozone fails to fulfil, or even approach, the optimum convergence criteria agreed by economists to be the minimum requirement for the efficient operation of a monetary union; crucially it lacks an adjustment mechanism to meet inevitably changing economic circumstances, both internal and external, other than price and income deflation; its governing institutions, the European Central Bank (ECB) and the European Commission (EC), are not subject to democratic accountability, let alone control; it was adopted for essentially non-economic motives as the next stage of an integrationist European project, but without the necessary political coordination to underpin it. Indeed, history demonstrates that all previous currency unions not supported by political union sooner or later collapse (Bordo and Jonung, 2000). Therefore, economic and monetary union (EMU) constitutes a 'leap in the dark' with potentially destructive implications if its participants are insufficiently cyclically and structurally convergence.

Hence, the connection between the operation of the euro and the recent worldwide economic recession simultaneously provide an illustration regarding the wider themes of this book in that national self-governance offers the potential for superior economic performance. Thus, we briefly look at the linkage between EMU as the key economic feature of the EU and ongoing repercussions of the financial crisis and recession.

The eurozone's fundamental structural weakness

These weaknesses are permanent, but become more damaging in times of crisis. In the wake of the worldwide financial recession highlighted by the collapse of the American investment bank, Lehman Brothers, in September 2008, the eurozone suffered a series of debt crises in individual member states. Greece and Ireland were thus afflicted in 2010 and Portugal in 2011, whilst markets are indicating similar problems in Belgium, Spain and, conceivably, Italy in the near future. To date, the eurozone's response has been piecemeal; ad hoc loans have been provided to Greece and Ireland, whilst minor revisions to the Lisbon Treaty were agreed to enable the creation of a government bail-out fund, the European Financial Stability Facility (EFSF), to become the European Stability Mechanism (ESM) from 2013. Such 'solutions' however, deal with the symptoms rather than the fundamental causes of the euro's structural weaknesses. The latter ensure that recurrent problems will emerge that vitiate proposed remedies once they affect a large member country. In the words of Gordon Brown (2010), 'these are not cyclical problems nor simply overhang from a world financial recession, but structural problems in need of a structural solution'.

Firstly, although the immediate origin of present discontents is usually located in the collapse of the Lehman Brothers; its antecedents lay in the bubble of speculative finance that occurred in the initial decade of the twenty-first century. This bubble was intensified by the pressure amongst eurozone countries in the preceding years for uniform interest rates to create an artificial monetary union that did not meet the required convergence criteria. Specifically, when the euro was introduced, the prevailing interest rate on 2 January 1999 stood at 3.25 per cent for the three month Euribar (Euro Interbank Offered Rate), whereby to achieve this target nominal rates fell significantly within nine years in France, Italy, Spain and Germany (O'Connor, 2009). Unsurprisingly massive foreign investment ensued, stock markets boomed, whilst house prices and household debt levels soared. Inevitably in such an artificially low interest rate environment, investment banks and pension funds sought greater rates of return from alternative asset classes. Consequently 'structured products' developed becoming the norm for investment in higher yielding loan assets.

Moreover, the strength of the euro until 2010 was determined by the competitive power of the German economy, which caused deflation in many other eurozone members since having the same interest rate for all countries with the euro as their currency created a 'boom-bust' cycle in a number of them. Hence, the growth rate across the zone languished, whilst unemployment as well as government financial and trade deficits multiplied. Additionally, in 2007 the German coalition increased value added tax by 3 per cent, which financed concessions to industry so that it could compete at a higher exchange rate intensifying the problems of its 'partners'.

Finally, the actions of the ECB as the institution responsible for the one-size-fits-all monetary policy in the eurozone also contributed to the perfect storm of events contributing to the crisis. Initially, it adopted an artificially low interest rate policy in 2002–03, which stimulated financial speculation, however, after 2005 it changed strategy so that rates climbed until the autumn 2008 crash; indeed it bowed to German pressure in June 2007 and as late as July 2008, raising interest rates to curb 'external inflation', despite an already tight monetary environment. Whilst few would claim ECB action to be the sole cause, it would be naïve to dismiss it as irrelevant rather than a contributory influence.

Although this series of events exacerbated the inherent problems regarding the functioning of EMU, such difficulties could have been tempered if it incorporated a more coherent adjustment mechanism to meet inevitably changing economic circumstances. In a dynamic market economy, characterised by technological and organisational progress, change is continuous; what Schumpeter (1942) famously termed the 'gale of creative destruction'. Furthermore, since the Industrial Revolution all capitalist economies experienced a cycle of periodic booms followed by periodic depressions. Consequently, it is crucial to the health of every economy that it possesses a robust adjustment mechanism to enable it to accommodate efficiently to the inevitable transformations that will occur in its internal and external environment. However, the eurozone lacks this crucial element in its structure.

Thus in the recent recession EU members no longer possess an independent monetary policy, so that they cannot set their own interest rate or their exchange rate to stabilise their economies. The current sovereign debt problems faced by several participating nations demonstrate the simultaneous dangers of losing control of their borrowing costs and the value of their currency to an external agency. Consequently, deflation with all its economic, political and social costs has become the eurozone's sole adjustment mechanism to the detriment of its citizens.

Conventional wisdom is that these contemporary crises are the product of deficient policy-making in the suffering countries, often expressed in moral terms as 'indiscipline' (Mills, 2011). In particular, budgetary policy has been too expansive and economies too competitively inflexible. The consequences of such errors are public expenditure cuts, increases in taxation and real wage falls. Additionally, the conventional wisdom also declares that once fiscal consolidation has occurred and labour market flexibility been introduced, the countries concerned can return to non-inflationary growth, as Germany did after 2003.

However, such conventional wisdom is misfounded, subjecting the eurozone to inefficient and ultimately unsustainable tensions. So long as the ECB tolerates weak demand in the eurozone as a whole and so long as the EU's founder members, especially Germany, run trade surpluses, it will prove impossible for less competitive nations to avoid insolvency. Their problems cannot be resolved by fiscal austerity alone, but only by a large rise in the external demand for their output. Indeed, 70 per cent of Germany's GDP growth between 1999 and 2007 was due to an increase in its net exports. In a eurozone without monetary or exchange rate offsets, any reduction in public expenditure generates at least an equivalent reduction in output. An attempt to cut a fiscal deficit by 10 per cent of GDP through falls in spending would involve an actual reduction of 15 per cent in GDP once declining tax revenues are taken into account (Holland, 1995). A diminution in purchasing power of this magnitude will create a spiral of debt deflation in which the cost of meeting unpaid debts leads to low growth, falling prices, loss of jobs and declining living standards as analysed by Minsky (2008). Such a scenario carries dire consequences for future productive potential, political dislocation and social distress (Baimbridge *et al.*, 1994).

Eichengreen (2010) compared the operation of the interwar years Gold Standard with that of the euro, arguing that both systems are undermined as much by persistent surplus, as by persistent deficit, countries. Indeed, more so because those in surplus are under no compulsion to change and are unwilling to contemplate this scenario. However, Germany now needs to return the favour, because the only way for other eurozone countries to lower fiscal deficits without their economies collapsing is through a huge net export expansion, based upon both improved productivity and crucially buoyant external demand. Currently neither is forthcoming such that it is difficult to regain competitiveness when the euro is strong, partly because Germany is so competitive and also eurozone inflation is low. Furthermore, markets are correct in questioning the will of governments and societies to suffer the enormous deflationary burden imposed by euro membership. This is also why the eurozone will only avoid the consequent deflationary effects by dismantling the reconstructing its entire mode of operation.

Potential remedies to the eurozone crisis

As to how this might be achieved, there are several potential routes of varying effectiveness and likelihood that appear available:

The normal initial response is that of **moral suasion**, castigating debtor countries for their profligacy. Such a shaming process may exert a limited effect, but is likely to be of only short duration given its illogicality; thus Germany is urging budget cuts on the Mediterranean nations, without acknowledging how its own surpluses were built partly upon their willingness to buy German commodities with borrowed money. If the euro is to prove permanent, it requires a firmly based equilibrating mechanism. Hence, the search continues for more secure foundations than the Treaty on European Union provides.

The provision of **ad hoc financial relief** usually subject to guarantees of changed economic policy, backed by market and political pressures, was the reaction to the eurozone crises during 2010 and the early months of 2011. As bailouts encompass, Greece, Ireland and Portugal, with market sentiment indicating the possibility of future loans to Belgium, Italy and Spain, a permanent source of funding is required. Consequently, eurozone members agreed to establish the EFSF to be replaced by the ESM after 2013, such that by 2017 the ESM will posses a fully paid-up capital base of €80billion, which provides it with a lending ceiling of €500billion, more than adequate to cover the cost of existing bailouts.

However, the gap between the €80billion base and the €500billion ceiling is composed of guarantees from eurozone member states. Calling upon these guarantees could be problematic; some countries may be financially unable to meet their obligations (e.g. Italy), whilst others may be politically unwilling (e.g. Germany). Therefore the formation of the ESM merely postpones the eventual clash between the irresistible force of eurozone-wide crisis resolution with the immovable object of national democratic decision-making. Already in Brussels during the last week of March 2011 police were compelled to fire water cannon at protesters who felt that austerity is being imposed without any democratic backing, to please financial markets. Never has the EU's political elite been so removed from its citizens due to the unaccountable operation of the single currency, nor so fragmented as its constituent economies diverge rather than converge as so confidently yet so erroneously hoped before its establishment. Hence, the current spectre of short-term financial assistance to less competitive participations as a quid pro quo for following long-run damaging deflationary policies may provide an immediate palliative, but can only postpone the eurozone's eventual demise.

Fiscal federalism is increasingly muted where, to quote one famous instance, the former German Chancellor Helmut Kohl asserted that without political union the euro was just a 'castle in the air'. Indeed, Bordo and Jonung's (2000) analysis of the history of currency unions that are unitary states supports his conclusion whilst all areas utilising the same money are currency unions. However, as Mills (2010) argues the difference between unitary states and associations of several is that the former are more internally cohesive, making it possible for their governments to (at least substantially) even out economic differences within them. MacDougall (1992, 2003) demonstrated that such a redistributive federal fiscal structure requires an EU budget in excess of its present 1.1 per cent of EU GDP, however, even his recommendation of 5–7 per cent of EU GDP is likely to prove inadequate compared to the minimum 20–25 per cent of GDP that federal systems usually necessitate (Baimbridge and Whyman, 2004). Without such redistributive funds, the cost bases of constituent economies become so unaligned that currency value adjustments are essential; thus Mills (2010) showed that labour costs in Spain are 15 per cent and Italy are 18 per cent higher than in Germany, compared to 2005, illustrating the magnitude of divergence between eurozone members. Thus, when the inevitable changes in exchange rates follow, the currency union dissolves.

Advocacy of fiscal federation to prevent break up possesses theoretical coherence, but ignores political reality. German doubts about extending the EFSF's proposed capacity would be multiplied in the face of fiscal federal problems. Indeed, currently David Cameron is attempting to move in the opposite direction by building a coalition of members to limit the EU budget to no more than 1 per cent of its GDP between 2014 and 2020. Additionally, to consolidate the euro, further harmonisation of economic and social problems may be necessary, but its political acceptability will be hard-fought and grudging amongst many participants. Therefore, its development is likely to prove problematic and, if it occurs, will be a lengthy process unable to alleviate contemporary dilemmas. It also intensifies long-held fears about the diminution of national sovereignty involved in closer integration (Redwood, 1997). Such an attack upon the independence of nation states, substantial even by MacDougall's calculations that are likely to prove underestimates, camouflages the fact that the single currency project was ill-thought through.

The current state of opinion was aptly summarised by analyst Stephen Lewis of Monument Securities (2010), 'there has to be a mechanism for automatically shifting resources from the stronger countries to the weak: a United States of Europe. The only problem is no one would want to part of it.' Thus, here lies the completely predictable origin of recent and future eurozone crises. A possible further response, as yet unarticulated, thus requires scrutiny.

The creation of a clearing union suggested by Keynes (1942) on an international basis during World War II could not only remove the sovereign debt problems of particular countries, but more significantly in the long term restore international confidence in the single currency. Currently, fund managers in the USA and Asia suspect that the euro's future is limited, so that they are divesting. Keynes' response to such problems rested on analysis of the operation of the gold standard, which failed because adjustment to imbalances, as in the eurozone, was compulsory for the debtor but voluntary for the creditor.

His solution was that all international transactions, giving rise to surpluses and deficits in balance of payments positions, were to be settled through clearing accounts held by member central banks at an International Clearing Bank (ICB). Member central banks would buy and sell their currencies against debts and credits to their accounts at the ICB, whereby these balances would be held in bank money (the bancor). Each member central bank would have the right to an account of bank money, essentially an overdraft facility, determined by its index quota calculated at half the average value of its country's total trade for the five previous years.

The object of the ICB was to maintain balance of payments equilibrium between each member and the rest of the world, whereby credits and debits would be created respectively by surpluses and deficits, which would be extinguished by their liquidation. Through this design, Keynes sought to create a simultaneous pressure on both surplus and deficit countries to 'clear' their accounts. Additionally, a central bank whose annual overdraft averaged more than a quarter of its index quota would be required to reduce the value of its currency by up to 5 per cent and to prohibit capital movement exports, whilst interest would be charged on overdrafts, rising in line with the debt-quota ratio. Moreover, similar provisions existed to liquidate surpluses such that any member in persistent surplus would be required to revalue its currency in steps of 5 per cent to release any sovereign-owned balances and investments, together with paying 5–10 per cent interest on credits running above a quarter-and-a-half of its quota to the ICB reserve fund. Furthermore, credit balances exceeding quotas at the end of each year would be confiscated and transferred to the reserve fund. Consequently, if all countries were in balance at the end of the year, the sum of bancor balances would be zero. Keynes also emphasised the importance of transparency, whereby the ICB provides 'an automatic register of the size and whereabouts of aggregate debtor and credit positions respectively. The danger signal is shown to all concerned.'

Therefore, Keynes' central idea was 'the establishment of a currency union based on international money accepted by all members for the purpose of setting international balances'. At first sight, the eurozone appears to meet this definition within its geographical area application. However, it lacks the underlying equilibrating mechanism to eliminate both deficits and surpluses recommended by Keynes. Moreover, his measures for debtor adjustment unlike those of the eurozone 'do not include a deflationary policy ... having the effect of causing unemployment'. They also possess the major advantages of redistributing resources within the zone without the political encumbrance of an apparatus of fiscal union, whilst addressing the problem of private, as well as public, debt.

However, the difficulties of securing the acceptability of long-term resource redistribution within the eurozone remain immense. Despite its overwhelming economic and social advantages over the contemporary deflationary alternative, in terms of the lost output and employment and associated costs imposed by the latter, surplus countries are unlikely to accept a loss of funds easily, other than as a 'one-off' response. Germany's recent political and legal manoeuvres to limit its liability demonstrate the magnitude of the task ahead for those who want to preserve the future viability of the euro.

Consequently, advocates of a single European currency face a fundamental dilemma. The present operation of the eurozone lacks the equilibrating mechanism essential for its long-run sustainability. However, the responses of moral suasion and the provision of ad hoc financial relief are plainly inadequate, whilst fiscal federalism and the creation of a clearing union lack political acceptability. Thus, so long as this state of affairs persists, consideration must eventually be given to a fifth response, albeit unacceptable to conventional wisdom; the collapse of the euro.

The **demise of the euro** would impose fewer costs than the status quo or alternative scenarios. Moreover, these could be minimised if it was accomplished through an orderly process, which would involve internal euro devaluation in each of the debtor economies, accompanied by capital and exchange controls on all external transactions until new non-euro currencies have been established. The main problem facing such a policy arises from the substantial cross border lending that has occurred within the EU over the last decade encouraged by its authorities, which will leave many banks carrying large losses. Therefore the key requirement becomes stopping banks from defaulting on their deposits, which would involve widespread public ownership and support of banks, whilst the ECB concentrates its borrowing power on securing bank liabilities. The optimum course of action for the EU economy and for the rest of the world inevitably affected by its performance would be for its authorities to engineer a managed dissolution of the eurozone immediately, whilst the borrowing power is still available to prevent banks from defaulting on depositors. However, the EU establishment currently possesses no such plans because it is desperate to prevent a eurozone break up, which it perceives as a calamitous setback for its basic project of ever closer union between members states. Ultimately, however, the pressure of events propelled by the lack of a eurozone equilibrating mechanism will prevail.

Conclusion

It can be seen that the construction of a single European currency never satisfied any of the proposed economic conditions for its establishment in relation to the Maastricht convergence criteria, the UK Treasury tests and Optimum Currency Area requirements (Baimbridge *et al.*, 1999). Rather its formation was driven by the assumption that a shared currency would generate economic convergence and political unity. Instead, it has achieved the opposite as increasing divergence amongst members undermines eurozone performance and threatens the economic stability of the rest of the world.

The extreme deflationary strategy now being imposed upon the least competitive eurozone countries carries frightening implications. The Club Med governments can slash their budget deficits only at the cost of huge falls in current economic activity and a substantial loss of future productive capacity. However, without the possibility of devaluation, they cannot hope for big export gains or even the capital inflows. Instead of the broadly Keynesian policies that revived growth not only in America and Britain, but also in France and Germany, these weaker members of the eurozone are being forcibly encouraged by the EU to pursue measures guaranteed to prolong and deepen their recessions. To make matters worse, Germany is planning to reduce its own budget deficit and to rely for the next phase of its recovery on export-led growth, which can only eliminate even more Club Med businesses unable to compete against German goods.

The EU leadership's priority is to prevent the single currency collapsing, but such a stance poses immense danger since the EU possesses only a limited volume of borrowing and political will (Mills, 2011). If these become exhausted in providing loans to preserve an unsustainable future for the eurozone, insufficient financial firepower may remain to prevent bank defaults when a number of countries decide to leave the single currency and devalue. This risk has been intensified by EU encouragement of cross-border loans within its jurisdiction, thus leaving European banks more exposed than they would otherwise have been.

Consequently, the more loans are denominated in German-backed euros, the greater the probability that these liabilities are inflated by devaluation. For instance, if banks owe €100billion before the currency depreciates by, say, 50 per cent, then the liabilities in the devalued currency double in relation to their original size. However, the longer the EU extends additional loans to preserve the status quo, the bigger divergences between member economies will become. Consequently, the sums of money owed abroad by banks in vulnerable economies can only become larger and the worse the eventual crash will be, as unemployment soars, businesses fail and the whole eurozone spirals down in debt deflation. This is truly a Greek tragedy, with devastating economic consequences for the people of Europe and indirectly for the rest of the world. Only the dismantling of the eurozone in its present form can bring ultimate relief.

CHAPTER 6

ALTERNATIVE RELATIONSHIPS

LOOSENING THE TIES THAT BIND

Introduction

The relationship between the UK and the EU has always proved to be difficult, juxtaposed between periodic elite-level enthusiasm for closer European economic (if not political) integration and a general lack of enthusiasm for such measures on behalf of a majority of the electorate, as indicated by successive opinion polls. Thus, Aspinwall (2003:146) is correct in his assertion that 'the question of whether to sacrifice domestic autonomy in favour of European integration is one of the most volatile and passionately discussed issues in British politics'. There are many inter-related reasons that may explain this phenomenon. Political and business elites are likely to benefit the most from economic and political integration, with the creation of a host of new career opportunities created due to the formation of new supranational regulatory and representational structures, whilst transnational corporations benefit from economies of scale available from larger markets, and their activities less subject to overview and control.

However, the evidence presented in this study demonstrates that, on balance, EU membership, and the momentum towards further political and economic integration, has tended to weaken UK national interests. The costs of EU membership have been found to exceed those benefits that have accrued to the UK, and the impact of participation in EMU would likely further exacerbate this economic deficit. In spite of this, all mainstream British politicians assert, regardless of the weight of evidence, that no viable alternatives exist to the strategy of remaining 'at the heart of Europe'. However, it makes little sense to allow a nation's democratic self-determination to be undermined through participation in further initiatives leading towards deeper economic and political integration without first considering a range of alternatives that exist for the UK, and that may facilitate more economic prosperity coupled with enhanced democratic accountability via the national parliament. This chapter outlines a number of these policy options and seeks to briefly evaluate their potential.

The status quo position

This is the most obvious alternative short-term position, whereby the UK retains EU membership but relies upon its opt-outs from EMU and refuses to participate in further economic and political integration. The maintenance of a national veto over economic proposals (i.e. taxation) remains a consistent feature of UK government policy towards the development of the EU, irrespective of the composition of government. Moreover, there are a number of precedents where individual member states have continued to pursue their individual national interests even if this threatened to hamper the effectiveness of the EU institutions. For example, Italy delayed the successful conclusion of the 1994 Edinburgh summit over a dispute concerning their milk quota, whilst the French refused to permit the creation of additional European Parliament seats until the new European parliament building was located in Strasbourg. Indeed, de Gaulle at one point utilised the negotiating tactic of the 'empty chair' to prevent the unanimity needed for decisions to be taken until other EU member states accepted key French demands.

The extension of qualified majority voting (QMV) has weakened the potency of this tactic somewhat, in recent years. Nevertheless, a determined effort may produce compromises. The key question to be resolved, if adopting this approach, is to determine whether the ultimate goal involves the non-compliance with future integrationist initiatives, which other nation states are free to pursue if they so wish, or an attempt to roll back the momentum leading the EU towards deepening economic and political integration. In other words, consideration must be given to whether the strategy is to create a multi-dimensional, Europe 'à la carte', or to press for the re-empowerment of the European nation states.

A second question, to be resolved if adopting the status quo strategy, relates to Britain's ability to establish a bilateral trade agreement with a third party, even if this related to an alternative trade association. This may involve closer ties with the North American Free Trade Association (NAFTA) and/or Commonwealth countries. These options are explored in more detail later in this chapter, on the basis that Britain forms these alliances subsequent to withdrawal from the EU. However, the point at issue in this section is to explore whether these potential trade advantages can be secured without the need to reject EU membership, and it would appear that such actions are indeed compatible with current EU rules. For example, Denmark negotiated an agreement with fellow Nordic states, which permitted the free movement of people, goods and services despite the fact that Norway, Sweden and Finland were not at the time members of the EU single market. This precedent does not, however, apply to the establishment of *new* unilateral trade agreements post-EU membership, but rather applies to the acceptance of *existing* trade agreements at the time of a nation's accession. Consequently, the benefits arising from closer co-operation with other trade blocs might cause difficulties within the constraints of EU membership.

These problems would, however, be in the most part political and not economic in nature. The practicalities of the UK being a member of two trade organisations are relatively easy to reconcile, requiring that all imported goods and services bear the mark of the country of origin, to prevent differential tariff rates creating a market for arbitrage in order to avoid paying higher rates of import taxation. Objections that such labelling is contrary to a single EU market can be dismissed due to precedents created by the solution to the BSE beef health crisis, whereby beef exported from Britain will have been labelled according to the country of origin to facilitate consumer choice. Once labelled according to the country of origin, if re-exported from the EU to US (or vice versa), the correct tariff charge could be applied when it enters the final market.

This strategy rests upon the premise that maintaining EU membership at its current status is both desirable and tenable. It maintains UK access to the SIM and provides the forum for participation in the determination of harmonised trade rules that define the marketplace. Yet, it avoids probable additional costs implied by EMU and moves to further limit national sovereignty through extending QMV. Moreover, it is perhaps the easiest position for politicians to defend, since it means doing nothing new and therefore avoids offending any section of their own parties.

The above is, however, at best a compromise solution. While further integration measures can be vetoed, and the UK can avoid participating in future experiments that may damage its economic potential, it remains committed to those that already exist. Apart from the obvious direct costs associated with the CFP and CAP, being a net contributor to the EU budget, together with the long-term trade deficit with other

EU member states, disadvantages include the net budget contributions, continuing trade deficits and the fact that, technically, the UK has an opt-out only from the final stage of EMU (i.e. having to accept the single currency) but not from earlier stages including the requirement to meet the convergence criteria established in the TEU. These require the UK to maintain inflation rates no higher than 1.5 per cent above the lowest three participating member states and interest rates no higher than 2 per cent above the average interest rates set by the same group of countries, budget deficits no higher than 3 per cent, and government debt no higher than 60 per cent of GDP, respectively, and finally a requirement for stable exchange rates pegged to other member states through participation in the Exchange Rate Mechanism (ERM). Thus, the UK would be economically tied to a slow growth area, and be required to implement deflationary policies perhaps unsuitable to the particular requirements of a recession or wider national interest. Moreover, recent demands made by the EU Commission that Britain reduces public spending, at a time when the international economy was particularly sluggish and government spending provided one means of stimuli to the domestic economy, was contrary to the preference specified by the British electorate in the 2001 general election in addition to being economically illiterate.

Furthermore, the Treaty of Rome obliges member states to allow the free movement of goods, services, capital and labour. Whilst in many circumstances the inhibited movement of goods and services is preferable, prevention of imposing even temporary restrictions upon the free movement of capital and labour may have greater consequences. The current controversy over a potential influx of individuals of working age from new EU member states highlights one possible problem area. Control over a national labour market is made more difficult, with the consequence that migrant labourers could place additional stress upon national health and social security systems. Moreover, they might provide a pool of exploitable labour and thereby undermine the competitiveness of 'good' employers who comply with minimum wage legislation and provide satisfactory levels of health and safety, and in the process cause episodes like the Morecambe Bay Chinese cockle-picker tragedy. Similarly, although the unimpeded movement of capital is conventionally assumed to be desirable, it can be destabilising for an economy that is damaged by a flow of 'hot' capital searching for a temporary profitable haven. Recent examples of Mexico, Brazil, Russia, and the 'Tiger economies' of South East Asia, all demonstrate the tremendous chaos that financial speculation can cause. Yet, the fundamental rules governing the EU would prevent a nation state from imposing restrictions, even if this was purely temporary, in order to prevent the disruption caused by speculative attack.

One further example involves EU rules prohibiting industrial subsidies because, whilst this is generally considered to enhance competition 'on a level playing field', there are circumstances in which the national interest may be served by such policies. One example might relate to facilitating the development of emergent technology, where future income streams are uncertain and therefore private financial markets either do not provide sufficient finance, or else reduce investment in the sector through demanding large risk premiums. A second example might relate to the emergence of an infant industry, which has the potential to grow into an internationally competitive venture, thereby enhancing the future prosperity of the UK economy, but which might be swallowed up by more established competitors in its early stages of development. A third case might relate to a nationally significant sector of technology, such as aerospace or the maintenance of a national car industry. It might involve support for space exploration, on the basis that the scientific and technological advances this might produce will enhance the competitive position of the national economy. Or it might be for reasons of national prestige, by keeping Concorde flying, for example, and thereby reminding consumers in other nations that British industry can produce products simply years ahead of their time; hence, raising the prestige of the 'Made in Britain' brand identity.

The status quo strategy may facilitate an 'à-la-carte' or 'variable-geometry' form of EU membership so that individual member states only need proceed with measures they favour and thus nations move at different speeds or even in different directions. Thus, a small number of EU member states could establish ever-closer political and economic integration between themselves, perhaps even resulting in the formation of a single, federal state, whilst other EU member states do not need to follow this initiative, and might alternatively wish to reallocate certain functions back to the control of local, regional or national governments through the principle of subsidiarity. However, whilst this scenario is popular in the UK, it is unlikely that supporters of federalism will easily acquiesce to the implied repatriation of powers to nation states.

Renegotiation of EU membership obligations

A second option available to the UK is to press for renegotiation of the obligations posed by membership of the EU. This would have the potential for resolving many of the issues that have generated the greatest costs for the British economy. It would involve withdrawal from some or all of the EU's drawbacks, for the British economy, whilst remaining within the organisation. Thus, targets for renegotiation could include the reconstitution of the CAP and CFP, renegotiation of the UK's budgetary contribution, together with opt-outs from specific policy initiatives (i.e. EMU, European foreign and defence policy, etc.).

This option has a number of precedents, including John Major's negotiation of an opt-out from the final stage of EMU (i.e. Britain remains bound by the TEU rules but is not compelled to take the final step and replace sterling by the euro-currency), together with the budget rebate that Margaret Thatcher forced from reluctant partners in Fontainebleau in 1984. Moreover, the current preoccupation with the establishment of an EU Constitution and institutional reform, in advance of the further enlargement of the EU, demonstrates a degree of flexibility in redesigning the organisation to limit its generosity to new entrants. This process will, if completed, significantly change the character of the organisation and modify existing arrangements established by international treaty. Thus, it is possible to secure renegotiation when the incentives are sufficient to encourage widespread compliance. Nevertheless, the requirement to achieve unanimity makes a general renegotiation difficult. For every advance secured by the UK, in reducing one of the various burdens on the British taxpayer, this financial cost will be redistributed amongst the remaining EU member states, and not surprisingly they are likely to be reluctant to accede to domestic unpopularity without some sort of trade-off.

One obvious source of negotiating strength for a British renegotiation derives from the fact that the UK is a net budget contributor and would probably remain so even after further contribution rebates and/or opt-outs from specific programmes had been achieved. In addition, the remaining member states enjoy the benefit of a large trade surplus with the UK, and therefore leverage might be forthcoming if renegotiation was pursued as the least disruptive alternative to full withdrawal from the EU. For this strategy to work, the threat of withdrawal would have to be credible. Indeed, the more Britain debated withdrawal, and the greater the public popularity of this option, the greater the concessions a government might be able to secure from other EU member states.

The renegotiation strategy need not necessarily isolate Britain from all other member states. Proponents of the strategy argue that a loosening of the ceaseless pursuit of increasing integration will be popular in other nations, particularly in Denmark and possibly

Sweden, where small populations proud of democratic achievements are unwilling to have this diluted into mass electorates too large to canvass personally and therefore increasing reliance upon a media-based campaign largely isolated from the electorate. Thus, the renegotiation strategy could be pursued in isolation or as part of an attempt to redesign the format of the EU at a more fundamental level.

Weaknesses with this strategy include its reliance upon the maintenance of negotiating strength and/or the ability to secure concessions written into international treaty. Otherwise, pressures might cause periodic challenges to any successful renegotiation in the way that the French government has periodically challenged the British budget rebate. It is also based upon the premise that concessions can be secured through negotiation. However, the enlargement of the EU, and increased pressures on the EU budget that this might bring, would increase the difficulty of this proposition. Indeed, the conception of a significant number of member states casting off current obligations would be more difficult to achieve than appeasing a single recalcitrant nation. Furthermore, all of this presupposes the achievement of some sort of compromise that, inevitably, implies that Britain will not secure all of its preferred objectives, and that some costs are removed from the British citizens at the detriment of enshrining others more deeply in the new arrangements.

Creation of an Associated European Area (AEA)

One interesting proposal that Britain could pursue as part of a larger renegotiation of obligations to the EU, made by Conservative Member of Parliament, Bill Cash, involves changing the rules to facilitate the creation of an Associated European Area (AEA). This would provide a distinctive choice in the type of European integration and pan-national, regional collaboration—pursuit of ever-deeper integration via an inner core group of EU member states, and a looser, co-operative arrangement between members of the AEA. The former could pursue their goal of creating a united states of Europe, complete with single currency, single central bank and convergence of economic policy, together with other trappings of a nation state, such as a federal president, foreign policy, police force, army, flag, parliament, passport and national anthem. At the same time, members of the AEA could continue their co-operation with the 'fast track' countries in trade and environmental areas, but retain national control over other areas of policy such as macroeconomics, currency, social policy, labour market, foreign and security policy. It would remove the requirement that each member of the EU has to accept the *acquis communitarie* (i.e. the existing rules and regulations agreed by existing member states) in full upon membership. This innovation would require modification of Article 43 of the Amsterdam Treaty. It would, additionally, restore authority to national parliaments, by removing the requirement of qualified majority voting from those areas of EU business where this currently applies. Nevertheless, it might prove possible because it would simultaneously release the impediments to a small group of countries accelerating their integrationist agendas, whilst providing nations with their preference of a looser arrangement through association.

In the Cash proposal, the AEA initiative is perceived as a means of securing more than simple renegotiation of EU membership commitments, however, because it is viewed as a means of forging a bilateral free trade agreement with NAFTA and used to challenge the customs union lying at the heart of EU economic arrangements, and its replacement with a free trade area. Therefore, this more far-reaching interpretation of the AEA has more than a degree of similarity with other options highlighted in this and the following chapter. However, in so far as the intention is to release Britain from most of its obligations imposed by EU membership, but retaining membership of a trade-bloc through the single internal European market, this might be more easily achieved through membership of the already-existing European Free Trade Association (EFTA) and European Economic Area (EEA). Rather than having to create a new institutional arrangement, Britain could make use of existing structures, agreed by the EU, to fulfil its goals.

Membership of the single market through EFTA and the EEA

This strategy would involve the UK formally withdrawing from the EU and re-joining the European Free Trade Association (EFTA) that it helped found four decades ago. In the process, the UK would be eligible for membership of the European Economic Area (EEA). Article 41 of the convention establishing EFTA states that any state may accede provided it receives the approval of the EFTA Council, or alternatively the Council may negotiate bilateral agreements with individual states subject to its unanimous approval by all member states. Article 42 establishes the right to withdraw from the convention after 12 months advance notice. Similarly, Article 128 of the EEA Agreement states that any European state becoming a member of EFTA can apply to the EEA Council to be party to the agreement, with the terms and conditions subject to negotiation. All future EU members are required to apply to become party to the agreement.

The EEA is an agreement made between EFTA (less Switzerland) to extend the internal market of the EU and that of the EFTA participants to create a trading area of 28 countries and some 462 million people. This is the world's largest and most comprehensive multinational trading area that came into force on 1 January 1994. Under the agreement, there is free movement of goods, services and capital across the entire area, whilst Article 28 provides for the free movement of persons and a single labour market across all member countries. Participants are encouraged to co-operate in the fields of environmental protection, social policy, education and research and development programmes. Exceptions to coverage include agriculture and fisheries, whilst the EEA has no common external tariff and therefore requires the identification of country of origin for all goods and services.

As a member of the EEA, the UK would possess full access to the SIM and retain some influence over the rules that affect trade with EU nations. The EEA ensures free trade without the discrimination against external nations created by a customs union. The terms of the EEA stipulate that the UK business sector would operate under the same general conditions as its EU competitors, whilst ensuring that EEA member states develop relevant legislation *jointly* without the EU imposing standards arbitrarily. The EEA provides member states with the right to oppose and veto EU law if they feel that it operates against their national interest. It also offers the possibility to participate in EU research projects and co-operation on the environment and the social dimension of EU legislation should any EEA participants find these beneficial.

A net transfer of income to the EU budget is part of the requirement for EEA membership, but it would be significantly lower than the high budgetary burden imposed by full EU membership upon UK taxpayers. Membership of the EEA also releases the UK from pressure to participate in the ERM, stipulated by the TEU and in eventual EMU. Given the UK's previous unfortunate experience of ERM membership, and the still larger disadvantages it would suffer through EMU, this constitutes a significant advantage. Thus, the EEA provides many of the advantages of EU membership without some of the costs.

Norway can be used as a precedent since their electorate rejected EU membership in a national referendum and yet was able to participate in the EU single market by means of the EEA. The EU have not sought to 'punish' Norway for failing to persuade its people to become full members, and on the contrary appear eager to take advantage of their addition to the single market to export goods and services, whilst having Norway pay a contribution towards the EU bureaucracy that manages the market.

One disadvantage of the EEA over full EU membership is that a power imbalance may arise between EU states and EFTA/EEA members, which could undermine many of the benefits that the agreement currently provides. However, if the UK reduced its membership to that of EEA status, this problem would be partially reduced in magnitude since the UK and Norway would jointly provide a far more credible counter-balance to the EU in future negotiations.

An advantage is that EFTA is a similar type of trade agreement to NAFTA in that it does not impose undue costs and restrictions upon member governments, barring those minimum rules necessary to maintain the effectiveness of the free trade area. The only significant differences are that the EEA is not as explicit on the issues of intellectual property and foreign investment, whilst it progressively adopts updated rules on trade harmonisation once these are agreed between the EU and EFTA members. Thus, UK membership of the EEA and NAFTA could establish closer co-operation between the two trade blocs around a two very similar free trade agreements.

Bilateral free trade agreement between EU and UK

One further option that the British government could consider relates to formal withdrawal from full EU membership and its replacement with a bilateral trade agreement between the EU and UK; sometimes referred to as the 'Swiss position'.

Since the UK is ill served by participating in the CAP and the CFP, a restriction of free trade with EU nations to industrial and financial goods and services would prove more beneficial than the present status quo. The remaining EFTA countries negotiated such a free trade agreement with the EU in 1972, after the UK, Denmark and Ireland had joined the EU, thus escaping from the financial burdens and policy constraints imposed by EU membership. As with membership of the EEA, this approach would allow the UK to reorientate its economic policy to serve its own perceived national interest rather than those of competitor EU countries. The money saved by non-contribution to the EU budget could be used to increase incentives for productive investment within the UK, and for state expenditure on infrastructural and research-based projects that increase long-term competitiveness. This option provides greater freedom than EEA membership, which implies the agreement of common rules and equal conditions for competition, so that greater pressure would be placed upon EEA participants to accept EU regulations to ensure continued co-operation.

Restricting EU relations to a free trade agreement would remove the possibility of such behind-the-scenes pressure.

The third option closely resembles Switzerland's current position, after a majority of its citizens and cantons voted against EEA membership in December 1992. This decision was motivated partly by a desire to preserve its 700 year independence from the rest of Europe, and partly by a disillusionment with an EU model which would undermine the country's tradition of direct democracy for a federation operated by an elite largely unaffected by its member states' citizens (*The Economist*, 28 November 1992). Although Switzerland's political and business elite favoured EEA membership, the Swiss voters did not agree. Indeed, in March 1995, a referendum voted to ban transit lorry traffic through the Alps by 2004 to force traffic onto the railways. Such democratically inspired national action to safeguard the environment was not welcomed by the EU.

These decisions did not haemorrhage economic vitality; instead they strengthened the Swiss economy. For instance, a sharp influx of foreign funds occurred after the 'No' vote, raising the stock market by 30 per cent and strengthening the value of the Swiss Franc. Moreover, Switzerland has managed to maintain relatively low levels of inflation, interest rates and unemployment, together with a significant balance of payments surplus, particularly when compared to the larger continental EU member states. Thus Switzerland is benefiting from its arms-length relations, despite a continued eagerness amongst its political elite for future EU membership. These relations are based upon over 100 bilateral treaties, including a 1972 Free Trade Agreement, which covers industrial goods (Church, 1993). Amongst OECD countries, agriculture apart, there is no economy more open to the outside world than Switzerland. Exposure to such competitive pressures encouraged the development of some of the world's most international-orientated companies. Switzerland is the fourteenth trading nation in the world and the second trade partner with the EU (after the USA) and the third supplier after the USA and Japan. Consequently non-membership of the EU has failed to hamper its economic development or its trading potential.

Despite economic success outside the EU, the Swiss authorities express two fears, which are familiar to UK citizens when confronted with the possibility of a change in relations with the EU. First, since the majority of trade is done with EU nations, membership may prove essential to protect it. Second, absence from the EEA may result in EU discrimination against Swiss-made goods through technical barriers. These concerns may be over-exaggerated. For example, in the Swiss case only 58 per cent of exports and 71.5 per cent of imports relate to the EU, so that its economy is less orientated towards the EU than most commentators claim. Additionally, like the UK, an increasing proportion of its international trade is being conducted with the fast growth areas in Asia and the USA rather than with the slow-growing EU. Thus Switzerland's dependence upon the EU market is likely to diminish in the future. The trend would be accelerated if the UK, Switzerland's fifth most important trading partner, left the EU.

In answer to the second point, the EU nations benefit far more than Switzerland from their trade so that they are unlikely to engage in discriminatory practices that could endanger their own more sizeable exports. Moreover, the Uruguay GATT (latterly WTO) agreement prevents arbitrary treatment of a nation's exports in any market, thus preventing active discrimination against Swiss, or any other countries', exports by the EU. Of course unofficial barriers to trade do exist, but EU membership is no guarantee that these will be dismantled.

Conclusion

The evidence reviewed in this book indicates that Britain's current relationship with the EU may have imposed net costs, not benefits, upon the domestic economy. Consumers pay higher prices due to the interaction of agricultural subsidies and budgetary mismanagement. Businesses pay the cost of over-complicated regulation and harmonisation growing out of the specific conception of a single market introduced amongst EU member states. Moreover, future costs relating to a low growth environment, deflationary economic policy infrastructure surrounding EMU and the introduction of the single currency, the euro, together with uncertain initiatives relating to the development of a social market, regulated labour market and aspects facilitating political unification (Baimbridge and Whyman, 2008). As a result, this chapter has outlined a number of potential alternative approaches to the relationship between Britain and the EU. Each possess advantages and disadvantages, and therefore government should make its selection at least partly on the basis of a cost–benefit analysis.

These alternative strategies possess a common characteristic, namely that they are designed with the UK retaining some degree of attachment with the EU. However, they would in all probability only mitigate against the pernicious effects of the EU. Moreover, they do not completely reflect the fundamental differences between the UK and its current EU partners in terms of economic structure, political and legal systems, let alone social and cultural identity. Therefore it is vital that the UK's future options for economic prosperity and democratic self-governance are not limited to these five alternatives or variations therein. Thus, the next chapter focus upon the alternative of withdrawal from the EU, and specifically how this could provide a number of new options for the British economy. Rather than withdrawal from the EU being a catastrophe, freedom from the restrictions imposed by over-concentration upon the EU could enable Britain to take an independent approach to political and economic issues confronting the nation, and adopt a global (not partial) world-view.

CHAPTER 7

BRITAIN OUTSIDE THE EU

Introduction

Successive British governments have sought to place the UK at 'the heart of Europe', and in the process have accepted the idea of the inevitability of a drift towards broader and deeper economic and political integration across a large swathe of the European continent. This is not to say that leading British political figures have not made personal stances against this process, together with a larger number who have argued for a loosening of the constraints imposed upon nation states by the integration process (Abbott, 2000; Benn, 2006; Gould, 2006; Mitchell, 2006; Owen, 2006; Redwood, 2000; Shore, 2006). Moreover, both Conservative and Labour governments have drawn their 'red lines' or vetoed specific new initiatives usually seeking to limit national self-determination. However, notwithstanding these efforts, the process of ever-closer unification has progressed from the trade-related common market, through the creation of a SIM, to the establishment of EMU.

Withdrawal from the EU provides one means of escaping these increasing constraints imposed by the EU upon the UK's economic behaviour, and which are not fully eliminated by those options involving retained EU membership. The status quo option implies similar costs to EMU unless the UK breaks the TEU convergence rules, for example, concerning ERM re-entry, whilst the EEA involves a budgetary cost and a general acceptance of the EU's regulations for the long-term survival of the agreement, which implies a de facto submission to the EU on many matters. Renegotiation could reduce many of these direct costs, but would be exceptionally difficult because a gain for the UK would involve a net cost for other member states. The Swiss option is the most palatable, but if this is achieved with the UK remaining bound by the Treaty of Rome then economic policy remains fundamentally constrained and speculators could therefore 'punish' Sterling for non-compliance with EMU rules. Therefore, in view of the varying but substantial costs implied by any form of EU membership, a further option for the UK is complete withdrawal, so that it can repatriate the ability to employ those policy tools it sees fit to better manage the country in its natural interests.

Withdrawal would take the form of parliament repealing the European Communities Act of 1972 under which EU directives take precedence over UK law, as well as the 1986 and 1993 European Communities (Amendments) Acts which added the SIM and the TEU. Following the example of Greenland, which left the EU after 12 years of membership in 1985, the UK could negotiate a Treaty of Separation to annul the Treaty of Accession and establish formal future trade co-operation on a mutually beneficial basis under the auspices of WTO rules.

Once attained, the UK is free to operate any economic policy it wishes. It could take the form of a determined effort to rebuild large sections of the UK's industrial base, decimated by EU, and accelerated by ERM, membership. Burkitt *et al.* (1992) outlined the essential elements of one such strategy. It could pursue a low-tax, market-orientated strategy, or else seek to stimulate growth rates through a combination of national Keynesianism, an active labour market and industrial policy. However, the crucial point is that UK citizens would possess the power to decide how they are governed and how the economy is run, rather than exercising merely a token vote at election time because important decisions concerning fiscal, monetary, exchange rate and trade policy are taken in Brussels. The economy would be free to react to external shocks in a way that suited its particular circumstances, not what suited Germany as the strongest EU state, or the 'average' member state, whether or not such a creation of statistical indexes actually exists! Indeed, as the German and Japanese economic 'miracles' were partially based upon a competitive currency and long-term low interest rates for industrial finance, the UK could adopt a similar approach to compete more successfully with EU members rather than be restricted by EU economic policies that are not in its interest.

Supporters of EU economic integration not surprisingly, dismiss the potential arising from renewed economic independence as illusory. They argue that sterling would be susceptible to speculative destabilisation once outside the ERM or EMU, requiring higher interest rates to be maintained than would otherwise be necessary, and thereby deterring productive investment. It has been further suggested that the only way in which the UK can exercise any power in world affairs is as part of the EU, because it is too small to do so on its own. Finally, withdrawal may endanger foreign investment in the UK and cause negative reactions from remaining EU members. Concern over these issues has effectively prevented detailed consideration of withdrawal as a viable policy option, even though this would prove popular with a large minority (and perhaps a majority) of the British population.

Far from the eurosceptics having won the battle of ideas, the reverse is actually true. Whilst opinion polls consistently show that UK voters do not like the EU, and would be free of it if they had a choice, the supporters of European integration control the agenda so firmly that whenever an opportunity arises to debate Britain's future, concern over the costs of withdrawal have obscured the best available evidence concerning the likely implications.

Many of the issues raised, however, enjoy little factual basis. For instance, after the ERM experience, it is disingenuous of the supporters of European integration to suggest that disengagement from the EU, and consequent floating of the currency, would damage sterling. During the two years of being fixed to the other EU currencies, the UK lost a total economic value of some £85.4–99.2 billion, equivalent to 8.2–9.5 per cent of 2004 GDP, which could have been devoted to productive ends. Moreover, it is unlikely to suggest that the world's financial markets will be fooled into believing that a permanently fixed exchange rate system will operate significantly better than the ERM, without inflicting permanent damage upon weaker EU countries and/or regions. International speculation does not occur against currencies set at the equilibrium level or against rational exchange rate systems but, as with the ERM in the autumn of 1992, it will undermine any moves towards EMU that are not viable, whatever EU politicians suggest. Destabilising speculation is best prevented by *international*, not EU, action, perhaps with a Tobin tax on currency transactions which are reversed within a short period of time, as suggested by President Clinton at the time of the ERM crisis (Tobin, 1994). The history of free floating currencies is not as successful as its advocates often claim, but managed floating is certainly preferable to the damage inflicted by an inflexible single currency.

The argument that the UK can only exercise any influence on world events within the EU is perverse, appearing to be simultaneously defeatist yet hankering for a world leadership role. The UK lost its former dominant world position because of economic problems. Decades of slow economic growth reduced the UK from the leading world economy before the turn of the century to a medium-sized economy in the 1990s, with political power declining accordingly. Japan and Germany obtained increased international influence not because of foreign policy or military might, but because their economic strength compels attention. If the UK is to regain influence, it must be based upon economic success, which is less likely to be secured within the monetarist-inspired EU-EMU policy straitjacket. Furthermore, the UK could secure international influence far in excess of its size through less conventional means. The Scandinavian countries, for example, achieved significant prestige for their environmental and human rights campaigns. The UK, when it established the National Health Service, was likewise a model that countless other countries used when constructing their own welfare systems. Likewise, the British democratic system is still admired by many sections of the globe as the 'mother of parliaments'. International influence does not, therefore, have to be of the traditional type. Even the latter can be more effectively attained through UK participation in the G7 summits than by being one voice amongst 27 (or more) within the EU.

The belief that withdrawal would reduce the flow of foreign investment into the UK is widely held, but a UK economy growing faster outside the EU with a permanently competitive exchange rate is more attractive to foreign markets than an EU member state. Foreign-based companies locate productive facilities in the UK to enhance their profits through producing output it can sell in the British and European markets, utilising the skills and abilities of a well-educated and flexible labour force. If firms remain profitable irrespective of British membership of the EU, they will continue to invest in the British economy in large numbers, as they currently do with few indications that the UK will participate in the most visible extension of European economic integration, namely the single currency.

Nor is the idea that withdrawal from the EU would provoke retaliation from current EU 'partners' any more probable. Apart from EU political pressure attempting to persuade the UK to change its mind, the other EU countries will not engage in a trade war because their surplus with the UK means that it would hurt them most. The UK habitually runs a large trade deficit with the EU, which means that they sell to us more then we sell to them. Consequently it would be self-damaging for the EU to engage in any measures that reduced trade with the UK. Indeed, if the UK could reorientate its economic policy outside the EU to promote greater economic growth, the UK would be able to buy more EU goods than if it stayed a member and remained a low growth economy within a low growth bloc. Thus the UK is in a strong position to bargain with other EU member states. Any impression of the UK as a weak nation, having to accept EU dictates, is a misconception propagated by the enthusiasts for further integration.

Withdrawal from the EU is only a first, necessary step. Once achieved, the UK can develop whatever trading relations with other nations it desires. It could remain non-aligned, taking advantage of the lower tariffs predominating in the world economy today, due to the success of successive GATT/WTO trade agreements. Or it can make alternative trade alliances. For instance, one possibility is to rejoin the European Free Trade Association (EFTA), so taking advantage of a free trade area without the pretensions of economic and political union. EFTA could be expanded to include those East European nations currently desperate to join the EU as a 'badge' of their market economy credentials, but which the EU is hesitant to admit because of the agricultural costs. An EFTA free trade area in manufactures, without agricultural protection, would assist all nations.

A second alternative could be to reinvigorate the Commonwealth trading bloc (West, 1995). Australia, New Zealand and Canada were severely damaged by the UK's decision to join the EU (Burkitt and Baimbridge, 1990) and subsequently reorientated much of their trade towards the emerging economies of east Asia. However, ties of language, culture and mutual advantage may ease a resumption of trade between them, other Commonwealth nations and the UK. The Commonwealth is an asset that the UK often underestimates, particularly since it now includes some of the fastest growing economies in the world, which often possess closer links with other fast growth areas than the UK. Consequently, reorientation of British trade policy will prove profitable.

A third alternative is to form an association with the North American Free Trade Agreement (NAFTA), which comprises the USA, Canada and Mexico (Baimbridge *et al.*, 2004; Philippidis, 2004). Since approximately one quarter of UK trade is already done with the USA, this bloc, together with the Commonwealth link to Canada, would be beneficial for the UK. Furthermore, talks between the USA, China, Japan and 15 other Pacific nations concluded with their determination to form a Pacific Free Trade Area by the year 2010 for the industrialised countries, which would encompass most of the fastest growing economies in the world. It may arguably be in the UK's economic self-interest to negotiate a trade agreement with such countries rather than to remain within the EU, since the potential for export sales is significantly higher. Consequently, whilst withdrawal from the EU provides the UK with an opportunity to operate an independent trading policy relying upon bilateral agreements with major trading nations, a combination of free trading areas between EFTA, the Commonwealth, NAFTA and in future the Pacific nations would create superior trading opportunities for the UK than remaining trapped within the EU could do.

Membership of NAFTA

If the UK were to join NAFTA, it would be required to leave the EU since the latter compels its member states to adopt a common external tariff and to subscribe to an EU-wide uniform external trade policy. There are, however, a number of compelling reasons why both the US and the UK should actively promote such a development.

As demonstrated, the UK and US economies are closely intertwined; further trade liberalisation would result in immediate benefits, in terms of trade creation, for both. From the past, the US and UK share a common culture and language, which make a contemporary trade relationship between them more likely to prove successful. A free trade area centred on an Anglo-American nexus is a more efficient fit than any conceivable alternative economic arrangement; it would also be building upon success, because over the past 15 years the US and Canada have created 2 million more jobs than EU countries.

For the future, the telecommunications revolution has led to the 'death of distance'; sharing borders no longer necessarily translates into increased trade and financial transactions, compared to a geographically distant country, as it has tended to do throughout history. A US-UK focal trading relationship would not work well in the era of the sailing ship or even when the Treaty of Rome was signed in 1957. Today information technology makes it eminently practical. If Britain joins NAFTA, the larger group will help to protect both the US and the UK from whatever outcome emerges from the EU experiment in supranationalism. A more broadly based NAFTA can counter the impact of either an imploding or a successful integrating, but by necessity largely inward looking, EU.

NAFTA countries have already expressed interest in establishing closer trading relations with EFTA and Chile. If Britain participated in such a grouping, a revamped NAFTA could ultimately be transformed into a global free trade association, which could potentially incorporate such countries as Australia, New Zealand, South Africa, the Caribbean countries, Denmark, Sweden, Norway, Ireland and Switzerland. It would be a grouping, based solely upon a commitment to free trade between them. It would seek no control of member states' trade relation with non-members nor would it possess the motivation to pursue 'ever closer union' that renders the EU unpalatable to many people within the UK. By contrast, NAFTA would prove more consistent with the democratically accountable sovereignty of each individual participating nation state.

One important factor for potential partners in a free trade area to consider relates to the degree of comparability of the economies in question. In particular, what possibilities for economies of scale exist for firms taking advantage of the larger free trade area, and whether trade creation will exceed trade diversion resulting from the creation of the larger trade bloc. The former benefit will result from companies currently stymied from expanding to their optimum size due to the limited size of the domestic market, and therefore are unable to offer consumers products as cheaply as would be the case in a larger market. This potential for lower prices will also be more likely realised in a larger market, where competition will prevent former national monopolies or oligopolies from exploiting their market power and maintaining high prices.

A second type of potential benefit accruing from the enlargement of NAFTA would refer to the degree of trade creation less diversion. This relates to the fact that, in a global market characterised by free trade, the most efficient producer(s) in a given commodity should specialise in its production, thereby optimising consumer benefits from low prices and efficient production. However, the existence of trade restrictions (i.e. tariffs) means that less efficient internal producers might be able to produce goods and services more cheaply, thereby transferring production from more to less efficient companies, and consequently wasting precious resources through this unwarranted diversion of trade. The benefit of a free trade area is where former tariffs levied on foreign firms now inside the tariff barriers might result in more efficient producers taking market share from less efficient domestic firms, thereby consuming less scarce resources and thus potentially increasing world production.

Since its withdrawal from the ERM, the British economy has been convergent, both structurally and cyclically, with North America. Consequently sterling tracks the US dollar not the euro, whilst its divergence from continental euro has widened. Thus sterling has fluctuated in a range of 13 per cent against the dollar since September 1992, but over a range of 37 per cent against the (former) deutschemark. Such oscillations determine the efficiency of interest rate harmonisation, leading to the conclusion that the American and British economies are more convergent with each other than either is with the eurozone. Such a conclusion is supported by analysis of the growth rates of the UK, the US, France and Germany.

In terms of business cycle, the UK has traditionally had a closer statistical relationship with USA than with Germany and other leading EU member states (Bayoumi and Eichengreen, 1993). Indeed, whilst the US and UK economies have enjoyed years of relatively rapid economic expansion, many continental EU economies have been trapped in conditions of slow economic growth and high unemployment. The US has created 22 million new jobs over the last decade, whilst UK unemployment stands at a 20-year low. Comparable unemployment figures for leading EU member states are 9.1 per cent in Germany, 11.7 per cent in France and 12 per cent in Italy, whilst standing at approximately 5% for the UK and US. Consumer confidence is high in both economies, and whilst America's output of goods and services has grown by an astonishing 58 per cent in nine years, Britain's economic growth rate has recovered to rank in the middle of the Group of Seven rich countries. Indeed, UK growth rates have outpaced those of Germany over the past two decades.

One noticeable change in both US and UK economies during the past decade has been the remarkable transition in their respective labour markets. The shift towards non-standard contracts, whether part-time, temporary or fixed-term working, together with the deregulation of the labour market, has increased the flexible adaptation of both economies to deal more effectively with industrial restructuring. One notable feature of this change is a decline in the non-accelerating inflation rate of unemployment (NAIRU), which denotes that level of unemployment, which is associated with a stable rate of inflation. If unemployment is forced lower, inflation accelerates; if unemployment exceeds this rate, inflation tends to fall. In a remarkable change from a decade previously, both economies have little tendency towards inflationary wage pressure despite low unemployment levels. Moreover, productivity has been rising quickly in both nations, with US productivity growth outstripping average wage growth. This, together with the high value of both currencies, has dampened remaining inflation pressure from increasing oil prices and property market booms.

One factor stimulating productivity increases, running at double the average of the previous 25 years in USA, is due to the impact of information technology. One estimate calculates that computers account for about a quarter of the overall increase in productivity, with increases in the use of information technology accounting for approximately half of this rise. The UK accounted for 44 per cent of all EU venture investment in high technology, with Germany a poor second with 17 per cent of the investment total. The diffusion of information technology and especially the Internet throughout the economy is incomplete, thereby allowing for continued high rates of future economic expansion (*The Economist*, 2000). Stock market asset expansion has further stimulated consumer expenditure, with high technology shares securing the greatest value accumulation, before more recent market adjustment.

Macroeconomic strategy is similar for the UK and US, with restrained fiscal policy enabling a greater role for monetary policy loosening to facilitate economic growth and increased levels of investment though lower real interest rates. Supply-side policy seeks to reduce taxation to encourage entrepreneurship, together with stimulation of investment in human capital. Consequently, both nations are ranked in the top 10 most competitive nations in the world; the USA maintaining its premier position. Moreover, amongst the most competitive EU nations, are the smaller, Scandinavian economies that tend to score well in the World Economic Forum international competitiveness index, with the larger, continental EU member states such as France, Germany and Italy receiving significantly poorer rankings.

A Commonwealth FTA

The greatest visible sign of economic weakness is the persistence of mass unemployment within EU nations, which is not matched by the North American, Asian 'Tiger' and Latin American areas. Indeed, it is interesting to note that many Commonwealth countries offer potentially faster growing markets than do other EU member states and hence the development of a Commonwealth free trade area.

Historic links with Commonwealth nations could give the UK a potential advantage in establishing trading links with these dynamic economies. These include Singapore, India, Pakistan, Malaysia, New Zealand, Australia, Canada and the 'new' South Africa. The East Asian link is potentially also important as a bridgehead to closer trading links with China. A survey by Price Waterhouse suggested that out of the UK's top 250 quoted companies, 31 per cent have already invested in China and a further 37 per cent expressed their intention to follow suit (cited in *Sunday Telegraph* 13 November 1994). In 1993, Commonwealth countries accounted for 12.8 per cent of all UK exports and 13.1 per cent of UK imports. Between 1991 and 1993 exports to the 'Tiger' economies, North America, Latin America and Eastern Europe rose by 53 per cent, providing two-thirds of the total export gain in this period.

Over the 10 years from 1983, £24.8 billion was invested in Commonwealth nations by UK companies, only £5.8 billion less than in the EU and half as much as in the USA, but nevertheless a significant volume for a trading bloc which receives little strategic attention compared with the supposed advantages emanating from the EU. This trade potential is likely to have become even more favourable as those regions with close Commonwealth connections out perform the IMF's estimated world growth rate of 3.7 per cent, whilst the USA, Eastern Europe and non-EU industrial countries were all anticipated to grow faster than the EU.

The World Bank (1993) estimated that the areas of the world that grew most during the past two decades, namely south and east Asia, will continue to expand more rapidly in the next decade. Additionally, growth potential is expected to result in significantly higher rates amongst most developing, than amongst the developed, economies. Latin America, Africa and the Middle East join Asia in offering UK companies superior potential for increased export sales than does the EU single market. OECD nations are expected to grow slower than developing countries, with EU members more sluggish than the rest of the OECD, so that the focus for UK companies wishing to expand sales overseas must be where demand is rising the fastest. Because of developments in the world economy, the danger of the single market is that it might distract UK firms from pursuing their widest options for sales and encourage a parochial European mentality at a time when a more international focus is indicated, for both short- and long-term trade prospects.

Since Asia and Latin America are the world's fastest growing economies, their purchase of world exports is also likely to increase. In 1993, one-fifth of UK exports, amounting to 4 per cent of GDP, went to developing countries. Because of the rapid growth of these economies, their share of exports will rise and become more important for UK economic development than the EU single market within a relatively short period of time. However, the UK is distracted from taking advantage of such export opportunities by the publicity given to the SIM and by the EU's common external tariff. The latter is an impediment to free trade which encourages other nations to place tariffs upon EU nations' exports, thereby putting UK exporters at a competitive disadvantage with the rest of the world.

Naturally enough, predictions relating to future market shares must always be taken with more than a degree of scepticism due to the tendency to fail to predict external, or even internal shocks, which may alter national growth and competitiveness figures substantially. Suitable examples concern currency and financial crises involving EU member states in 1992, Asian economies in 1997 and Russia in 1998.

Nevertheless, even including these effects, east Asia appears likely to expand more rapidly than continental EU economies over the next few years, and therefore trade relations are more likely to grow in importance over this medium-term time period.

A revitalised EFTA?

The possibility of using EFTA membership in order to access the SIM was discussed in the previous chapter. However, the potential offered by EFTA is worth exploring in the context of establishing supplementary trade relationships supplementary to those with the EU member states.

In this regard, a revitalised EFTA could provide an alternative to the EU as a looser form of co-operation between European nations. This might prove interesting for those political parties and segments of the electorate in nations currently waiting their opportunity to secure full EU membership. There is significant electoral opposition to European integration amongst a number of EU accession candidates, in addition to sizeable majorities within Norway, Sweden, Denmark, Iceland and Switzerland who are broadly sceptical towards further European political and economic integration. Many of these voters would certainly prefer the type of co-operative arrangements that could be forged through the auspices of EFTA than via the 'full-blooded' version pursued by the EU.

Conclusion

Concentration upon Britain's relationship with the EU is not, however, a sufficient response to the analysis contained within this book. Indeed, in part, it replicates one of the most fundamental problems that EU membership has imposed upon British businesses and government; namely, that it has forced an over-concentration upon the European region to the detriment of relationships with other potentially even more significant areas of the world. Indeed, it may have caused Britain to narrow its focus, and in the process to neglect previous significant partners in trade and commerce. It has caused too much of Britain's energies to be dedicated towards facilitating convergence with European neighbour economies, rather than concentrating upon developing markets for British goods and services amongst the fastest growing areas of the world.

This chapter examined a number of the main options available to the British economy following a decision to withdraw from EU membership, and its consequent freedom to craft an independent economic policy based upon national priorities and interests. This would allow a British government to design and implement an economic strategy irrespective of the rules and regulations arising from Brussels. It would additionally enable Britain to form new trade alliances with trade groupings or blocs that better represent the dynamic elements of the world economy. Rather than being tied into regional economic integration, as distinctive areas of British competitive advantage are sacrificed in pursuit of harmonisation across the European continent, British workers and companies could benefit from a change in focus—from a narrow, euro-centred vision of the future, to a global, more enriching alternative.

Withdrawal would free Britain from many of the regulations and standardisations imposed by the EU in the cause of creating a fully functioning single market. It would release a significant sum of money that the UK annually transfers to the EU budget (net of receipts), it would free the UK to adopt different trade policies with other nations and/or trade blocs throughout the world. Moreover, it would prevent unwelcome constraints being placed upon national macroeconomic management, from the rules governing EMU to those adopted in the very early years of the Treaty of Rome. However, it also has the potential to provide Britain with the *freedom to* develop alternative economic and trade policies that are distinctly different from those pursued by EU member states. It could promote reindustrialisation, using all of the instruments of industrial policy to select, support and nurture strategic industries through the early and unknowable stages of their development, until they too achieve their own international competitive advantage. Governments may prefer to make use of fiscal, monetary and exchange rate policy instruments, unhindered by EMU dictates, to prioritise economic growth, low unemployment and low inflation above external exchange rate stability and compliance with the dream of a 'united states of Europe'. This issue is considered in the next chapter.

CHAPTER 8

A NEW ECONOMIC POLICY FRAMEWORK

Introduction

Participation in further EU integration will place an additional straightjacket upon macroeconomic policy in the UK and increase the difficulty of pursuing national interest. For example, the model for EMU seeks to impose a particular institutional framework that restricts the flexibility of action of individual countries in order to enable economic policy to be determined, or at least co-ordinated, from the centre. Many economists (Jamieson, 1998; Michie, 2000; Minford, 2000; Ormerod, 1999) argue that greater autonomy for individual nation states, under the principle of subsidiarity, might provide a more stable economic environment in which to pursue further co-operation between countries. However, largely due to the political desire to tie members more closely together, the EU is seeking to progressively replace economic autonomy for a nation state with the requirement to co-ordinate its economic strategy with the EU norm, or else be subject to sanctions levied by the EU Commission (Pennant-Rea *et al.*, 1997).

A decision to reject such developments would restore to national government those economic instruments essential to the management of its economy. Governments will be able to devise different economic programmes and, once endorsed by the electorate, will possess the means by which to pursue their chosen objectives. Democracy will, therefore, be restored, so that citizens can once again enjoy the opportunity to choose the economic strategy pursued by the government of the day. Moreover, governments will be able to pursue a more balanced economic programme, pursuing the multiple objectives of full employment, high economic growth and a sustainable balance of payments as well as low inflation. The opportunities are substantial.

To illustrate the broad range of different policies that could be enacted, this chapter outlines a number of broad alternative economic strategies that could be pursued once a nation is freed from the restrictive grip of the ECB and the requirements of the TEU, let alone any future developments. Additionally, it discusses the development of complementary industrial strategy and exchange rate policy. The former can only prove effective if supplemented by fiscal and monetary policies that target growth and reject deflation. Inflation is not a British disease but the symptom of an economy that cannot produce enough to satisfy domestic demand. Britain's basic economic problem is insufficient production. The solution is to boost demand but channel it to UK industry, improving profits, stimulating production and hence productivity, and providing the incentive to invest; thereby cutting unit costs and inflation through a considered policy of economic expansion. It can be achieved, free from EU constraints, through control of the exchange rate and the accompanying interest rate changes. Such a policy makes it profitable to produce in the UK, by utilising the price mechanism to boost exports, encourage import substitution and lure British industry back into sectors it has abandoned, whilst a tax on imports would provide crucial support. An effective exchange rate policy is critical to the successful implementation of the outlined options for macroeconomic policy. The intention is to demonstrate, not only that national economic management is still feasible, but also that it is preferable to transferring the main levers of macroeconomic policy into the hands of the EU which is incapable of using them consistently in the best interests of all member states simultaneously.

Tight monetary policy/low interest rate strategy

The first potential economic strategy seeks to follow the framework established by Alan Greenspan and the US Federal Reserve Bank, whereby national monetary authorities (whether in the hands of an independent or democratically controlled central bank) seek a higher long-term growth rate by providing a favourable climate for industrial expansion through low inflation and hence reduced long-term interest rates. Fiscal policy is used to support the more dominant monetary policy by restraining inflationary pressures, thereby reinforcing the low interest rate objective. The globalisation of financial markets prevents governments from 'persuading' financial institutions to finance public sector borrowing at less than the market rate. Consequently, the higher the level of public sector borrowing on the international money markets, the higher the price for that borrowing in terms of long-term interest rates. This approach assumes crowding-out in the financial markets due to limited resources for lending to prospective borrowers because, were banks to create money simply to meet the additional demand for funds so that the supply of loanable funds was relatively elastic, interest rates would be unaffected. However, the strategy seeks to reduce government expenditure in order to reduce borrowing and hence interest rates.

In 'hard' versions of this strategy, the government endeavours to maintain a high value for the currency in order to squeeze inflation further. The objective is comparatively easy to accomplish if the country enjoys a trade surplus, because the pressure on its exchange rate is upwards due to the country's competitive position, assuming the absence of speculative motives to counter this fundamental relationship. However, since the UK typically suffers from a current account trade deficit, a rise in short-term interest rates is needed to attract sufficient short-term capital investment into UK securities to counterbalance trade-related downward pressures on the currency, thus maintaining a high value for sterling. However, these developments will impact upon long-term interest rates and thus conflict with the fundamental goal of the strategy. Nevertheless, there is no reason why sterling should not prove to be a stronger currency than the euro, particularly due to the participation of high-inflation southern European member states and an ECB forced to balance economic policy between conflicting needs (Baimbridge *et al.*, 1999; Weber, 1991). The ECB will require time to establish its anti-inflation credibility and to demonstrate that it can ensure the long-term stability of EMU.[1] Moreover, unemployment remains the greatest economic problem for Europe to solve; thus it is probable that, sooner rather later, the ECB will come under pressure to loosen monetary policy. The departure of German Finance Minister Lafontaine may have indicated an early victory for supporters of the independent ECB and the restrictive Maastricht rules, but it does not indicate which viewpoint will ultimately prove the stronger.

A fiscal-based strategy

A second distinctive economic strategy involves the more active use of fiscal as well as monetary policy in order to pursue both internal and external balance for the economy. Internal balance refers to more than just low inflation, but also to low unemployment and to high rates of economic growth. Accordingly, a mixture of demand-side reflation and supply-side labour market policies, particularly measures encouraging re-training and labour mobility, could reduce unemployment. Thus, the net stimulative effect is targeted upon specific sectors of the economy that most require assistance, rather than raising aggregate demand per se and creating inflationary bottlenecks. Economic growth could be facilitated by the maintenance of a competitive exchange rate through managed floating, perhaps based upon a trade-weighted basket of currencies, together with tax incentives for firms that increase productive investment. A mixture of fiscal and monetary policy could restrain inflation; if this proved difficult to achieve, rather than abandon the other internal objectives, governments could enact additional measures to restrain inflationary pressures. These might include the temporary re-introduction of credit controls, an incomes policy (tax-based or otherwise) or co-ordinated national bargaining. Although currently unpopular amongst economists who prefer the allocative efficiency of free markets, the reality of sticky wages and prices, due to oligopolistic markets as much as the existence of trade unions, gives rise to the possibility of market failure resulting in persistently high unemployment and slower-than-trend output growth. In this case, government intervention is justified to achieve a superior outcome. It is a fact that the majority of the world's nations still retain exchange controls to assist them to manage their economies, whilst Ireland's remarkable recent growth rates have been facilitated by 'social contracts' with trade unions to prevent wage pressures undermining its competitive position. Finally, external balance can be achieved through the provision of a competitive exchange rate, although structural problems in export sectors may require supplementary supply-side measures to improve product quality, reliability and to encourage a shift of resources to provide goods and services in growing rather than stagnant markets.

The 'Keynesian' strategy is notably different from the first approach due to its positive role for government action in wider areas of economic activity. Accordingly, an approach of this nature would be facilitated by an industrial policy designed to enhance the long run competitiveness of UK industry. An analysis of trade flows indicates that Britain enjoys a comparative advantage in financial and media services, and those areas of manufacturing which rely upon a high degree of scientific innovation, such as telecommunications, pharmaceuticals, aerospace, energy exploration and generation, biochemicals and computer-related activity.[2] In contrast, Britain is less competitive in lower value-added manufactures, most notably in engineering and metalworking sectors. Outside the EU, Britain could strive to strengthen its competitive position by enhancing the productive potential of already strong sectors through *targeted* reductions in corporation tax, research and development tax credits, and greater spending upon education. Innovative research undertaken by universities and publicly funded research centres requires prioritisation in terms of the allocation of government resources, if higher growth is to be forthcoming. Labour market programmes designed to re-equip workers for the requirements of industries with a competitive advantage ensure that their maximum growth potential is not undermined by the lack of a skilled workforce, whilst facilitating the shift of resources to more productive uses. The promotion of firms based in the UK has the further advantage that it will substantially improve the balance of payments position in the long-run, whilst ensuring that the majority of the improvements in living standards and profitability remain in the UK economy and are not repatriated abroad by transnational corporations. Moreover, the trend towards foreign-owned plants demanding ever-increasing 'sweeteners' to retain production in existing plants raises the possibility that providing inexpensive finance or development grants to UK-based firms might prove a cheaper alternative that generates an improved long-term growth reward.

An industrial strategy

An active industrial strategy must be based upon understanding of what promotes industrial competitiveness. Porter's (1990) exhaustive research demonstrated that economic success is achieved through the development of 'clusters' of mutually reinforcing internationally competitive industries. Britain once enjoyed the benefits of clustering, as one sophisticated industry spawned and reinforced others; British goods pulled British services into overseas markets and vice versa, its multinationals served as loyal customers abroad, and the cluster of financial services and trade-related industries was highly self-reinforced. However, a gradual unwinding of industrial clusters occurred, with only pockets of competitive advantage remaining. British firms rely heavily on foreign inputs and machinery. As some UK industries became uncompetitive, they were increasingly poor buyers for other domestic products. The spiral continues downward, cushioned only by long tradition and the remnants of technological innovation. Thus many British manufacturing companies lag behind those of other industrial countries such as Germany, Japan and Sweden in process technology and in their willingness and ability to invest in new plant, undermining competitive advantage in industries producing manufacturing equipment such as machine tools, process controls and lift trucks. In the car industry, for instance, the UK has lost competitive advantage in end products outside a small luxury sector and positions in the manufacture of a variety of automotive components eroded with it. The same process applied to an even greater extent in durable goods, such as appliances and consumer electronics.

The sectors where British firms sustain competitive advantage partly owe it to a cluster of related, supporting industries. In consumer goods and services, a vibrant retail industry creates pressures to innovate. Britain was among the first countries to permit television advertising, which created a fertile environment for companies to build skills in modern marketing. The City of London provides another sector where British strength relies upon the advantages of clustering. Britain's international position in financial services such as trading, investment management, insurance and merchant banking is concentrated in the City, along with supporting activities like information and telecommunications facilities, financial journalism, printing and publishing, legal services, financial advertising and public relations. The dynamism of this cluster attracts firms worldwide to locate in London.

However, British industry overall lacks dynamism and the ability to upgrade its competitive position unaided, due to cumulative disadvantages which reinforce each other negatively in the spiral of relative decline. Problems in one industry hurt others. Falling competitiveness reduces relative living standards, making consumer demand less sophisticated. Downward pressure on government revenue leads to cutbacks in resource creation and social services, weakening still more industries. Britain's remaining competitive advantages are insufficient to generate sufficient well-paid jobs for all its citizens. Therefore it is caught in the downward spiral of clustering and its relative living standards suffer accordingly. Loss of competitiveness creates its own momentum, which, once established, is hard to reverse without a major policy initiative. Indeed lingering market positions and customer loyalties allay any sense of urgency about the need for change.

A significant proportion of growth in skilled and value-added UK employment has occurred from investment by foreign firms. Much of this, however, is attracted by relatively low production costs. Foreign investments are largely in assembly facilities, taking advantage of poorly paid, mostly unskilled labour, or in service industries such as hotels, golf courses and retail outlets. While overseas capital benefits

British industry, an economy whose growth depends on assembly outposts of foreign companies will be constrained in terms of productivity increases. Certainly such investment alone cannot break the vicious circle between a weak balance of payments, slow growth and declining manufacturing, which has developed in the three decades since UK accession to the EU.

Britain demonstrates the problems facing an economy needing to restart the upgrading process. A number of fundamental problems must be tackled by a coordinated industrial strategy if recovery is to occur:

- The UK cannot regain innovation-driven competitiveness without a world-class educational and training system encompassing all socioeconomic and ability levels. The rate of investment in human skills must rise substantially, standards must be improved and technical expertise must be stressed. This is perhaps the most pressing issue facing Britain over the next decade, for the need to improve the quality and quantity of its labour force is great. Research conducted in France and Germany by the National Institute for Economic and Social Research (Prais and Wagner, 1988; Steedman, 1988; Jarvis and Prais, 1989) demonstrated that the level of technical qualifications of craft workers is far superior in those countries than that achieved in the UK. A further report (Jarvis and Prais, 1989) on training in the retail industry concluded that the UK was creating a certificated semi-literate underclass'. Moreover, training trends are deteriorating in the UK; in 1964 240,000 young people were in apprenticeships and 148,000 in industrial or mercantile training, but some 20 years later these figures had dropped to 55,700 and 36,700 respectively.

- British companies, as well as the government, face a busy skills agenda. They need to realise that without a broader pool of trained human resources, their competitive advantage will be limited. This need embraces managerial staff, where British firms have traditionally employed far fewer university graduates than other industrial economies. Unless companies accept greater responsibility for internal training of all workers, they will make little progress relative to their competitors. The multi-skilling of the industrial workforce provides the route to productive flexibility, quality and innovation, while enhancing individuals' occupational status. The inability of individuals to contribute to their full potential is reflected in the stunted economic performance of many sectors. Narrow vocational training is a contradiction in an economy that seeks to place workers at the forefront of innovation.

Consequently the emphasis must be on quality training to reflect new economic requirements.

- UK investment levels need to increase to match the improved labour force, primarily in manufacturing but also in the infrastructure of essential services. Machinery and plant in many sectors are currently antiquated, so that the development of advanced technologies as a basis for expanding into modern high value-added production is held back. The future competitive advantage of British firms can only be based on innovation in new products and new processes of production. Government aid to industry enabling the maintenance of high investment can play a crucial role in this process.

- The UK lags behind other industrial nations in the share of GDP allocated to research and development (R&D). Government investment in R&D is among the highest as a percentage of GDP across OECD countries, but half is focused on defence that possesses limited spin-offs for civilian industry. Even more troubling is the low rate of overall R&D spending in firms. A reallocation of both government and company resources towards commercial R&D is necessary to successfully reverse the spiral of relative decline, by stimulating both the generation and the diffusion of innovation. Supporting reform of the accounting treatment of R&D expenditure would also prove beneficial.

- Without sophisticated buyers, innovation and dynamism will be stunted. Britain already enjoys demand-side advantages in luxury and leisure-related commodities. The challenge is to upgrade industrial demand to broaden the sphere over which British companies benefit from well-informed buyers. Improvement of managers' and workers' education contributes to this objective. The prosperous London and South East markets can be the cutting edge of new consumer demand conditions.

- Some of the operations of London financial markets have become a barrier to British competitive advantage. Institutional investors often possess little commitment to companies nor do they play an active role in corporate governance. A group of large British conglomerates has emerged, who buy and sell unrelated companies, but whose financial orientation does little in the long-run to upgrade competitive advantage in domestic industry. The result of such trends is that US-style earnings pressures threaten to dominate UK management thinking. However, a long-run bias in industrial decision-making is in the interests of national prosperity.

- British economic prosperity will never be complete without a faster rate of new business formation to make headway in reducing unemployment, because revitalisation of established industries sometimes reduces the size of the workforce. However, new business formation depends on skills and ideas, on appropriate motivation and goals, on active competition, and access to capital. One of the urgent reasons for upgrading British education, especially in universities, is to seed new ventures. The UK cannot rely on foreign investment for job creation and prosperity (*The Economist*, 1991).

These measures should reduce the level of joblessness, leading to the long-term restoration of full employment. By reducing, and eventually eliminating, the long-run growth of imports and by stimulating an expansion in exports, the strategy aims to reconcile full employment with the simultaneous achievement of payments equilibrium.

However, such an industrial strategy can be reconciled with current EU regulations, let alone its future federal aspirations, thus Britain's essential interests' conflict directly with EU moves towards greater integration. However, with determination and imagination, there is no reason why Britain cannot acquire again the significant comparative advantages in the production of goods that once made it the workshop of the world. Services are a crucial complement to this process, but alone do not provide the growth momentum of manufacturing industry nor can they be relied upon to substitute for the deficits in overseas visible trade. The construction of such a competitive economy in the UK involves the complete unravelling and reconstruction of its relationship with the EU. It is to this relationship that we now return.

The policies required to revitalise British industry run counter to current EU rules and would be frustrated by movement towards economic and political union. Major historical trends cannot be reversed quickly; a permanent increase in the British rate of productivity growth, for instance, requires sustained economic expansion, a difficult endeavour given the deflationary tendencies of EMU.

UK membership of the EU tends to frustrate the achievement of these objectives through three fundamental mechanisms. Firstly, Britain's relatively weak competitive trade position with other EU nations prevents market forces from generating unaided the profits required for industrial regeneration. Experience demonstrates that market operations tend to accentuate strengths and deficiencies rather than eliminate them. Secondly, the Treaty of Rome severely limits aid to industry, whilst the public expenditure needed to complement the price mechanism in promoting industrial regeneration is circumscribed by the TEU convergence criteria and SGP. Thirdly, the current functioning of EMU limits the scope for discretionary national economic policies. Therefore, both markets and governments are prevented from addressing the UK's basic problems by the very essence of EU operations and developments.

The scale of deindustrialisation is uniquely intense in Britain requiring the implementation of a solution geared specifically to British problems rather than a more blunt, less sensitive EU-wide programme. However, any strategy designed to confront the UK's deep-seated trading crisis within the EU will take many years to come to fruition. Therefore a danger arises that such a strategy could be jettisoned before it has had sufficient time to be effective, in the face of short-term pressures. This consideration suggests that government funds for industrial restructuring should be exempt from any immediate requirement for reducing public expenditure. Consequently a programme to stimulate industrial investment, boost jobs creation, and improve the quality of education and training must be rigorously maintained in the face of potential short-run problems. The benefits from such a programme would be reaped over a five to ten year period, if the constraints imposed by EU integration are prevented from undermining its potential. Survival in the interim requires the creation of a breathing space for the British economy until the programme becomes effective. The preservation of this essential space depends upon the UK government possessing an active exchange rate and trade policy, with discretionary control over movements in the external value of sterling and freedom to pursue independent fiscal and monetary policies.

Exchange rate policy

Export-led growth occurs because the firms that are competitive in world markets commence with the advantage of costs at least as low as their competitors given that an economy is usually required to sell its output to the rest of the world at a competitive price. If it does so, it will embark on export-led growth; otherwise import-led stagnation is likely to follow. Moreover, once export-led growth is established a number of forces operate to keep fast growing economies moving ahead. Particularly significant is the impact of successive waves of investment, which tend to reduce the cost of goods in the internationally traded goods sector so rendering export prices increasingly competitive. However, a key determinant of competitiveness is to establish and maintain a competitive exchange rate, i.e. one that achieves balance of payments equilibrium at full employment.

If a policy of expanding the British economy through the export-led growth engendered by a competitive exchange rate is adopted, it is unlikely on the available evidence, to cause substantial inflation during its early stages. Indeed, it could lead to inflation falling. However, a further potential generator of price increases may be an overexpansion of domestic demand, so that the economy becomes overheated. Once demand exceeds the capacity to supply, prices begin to rise. Such a scenario must be avoided. However, these problems are not insurmountable; they can be contained through a variety of channels. First, the more resources that are deployed into sectors facing falling cost curves and engaged in foreign trade, the easier it is for self-sustaining growth to be achieved. Large returns on investment that can be obtained in these sectors can provide sufficient new profitability to finance additional new capital requirements. Second, for at least some shortages there is considerable scope for importing what cannot be obtained from domestic production. For many commodities there exists an elastic supply of foreign output to meet domestic shortages. Third, any attempt to reflate the British economy in order to achieve full employment has got to include an undertaking of training, retraining and education, particularly covering engineering and technical work. A competitive exchange rate cannot in itself be a panacea for all the UK's economic problems. It will take some years to recreate full employment. When the pound's external value ensures competitive exports, it will still require price changes to produce substantial increases in output.

Hence, over a period the desired objectives of exchange rate policy are short-term stability and long-term flexibility. The dangers to avoid are long-term fixity and short-term volatility. The only way of achieving these goals is a system that permits long-run change whilst avoiding violent short run fluctuations. Various policies are available to secure this end, but membership of the euro prevents them being implemented by establishing a permanent fixity which imposes deflation upon less competitive national economies. However, this does not reduce relative prices automatically; it does so by creating unemployment and stifling the future prospects for economic growth. That is what is meant by those who advocate EMU membership as a 'discipline' upon the British population.

The exchange rate between two currencies is a price like any other. Its movement enables the two economies to achieve trade and payments balance. If one country's exchange rate is over-valued its exports become more expensive in the foreign currency, while imports become cheaper in its own currency. Therefore export volumes tend to decline and import volumes to increase, so that eventually the trade balance moves into deficit and unemployment rises. Conversely, when a country lowers its exchange rate, exports became cheaper and expand, while imports are constricted. The trade balance usually improves but at some contemporary sacrifice of real income due to higher internal prices.[3]

The correct level for the exchange rate at any one time is that which enables an economy to combine full employment of productive resources simultaneously with approximate balance of payments equilibrium. A higher exchange rate generates overseas deficits and unemployment; a lower one leads to the build up of excessive foreign currency reserves and domestic inflation. However, it has been emphasised that this 'correct' exchange rate varies in value over time (Jay, 1990). The variety of influences affecting economic performance (trade balances, productivity, price movements, discoveries of natural resources etc.) combine to ensure that the 'correct' value of the exchange rate alters with the years. Therefore a country needs to retain its ability to adjust the external value of its currency. To fix it irrevocably forever is as difficult as attempting to maintain in perpetuity the rate of income tax or the price of oil. The endeavour to do so generates economic inefficiency, usually in the form of accelerating inflation or a rise in unemployment.

Consequently Britain's optimal strategy is to retain the national policy instruments required to increase its competitiveness in a socially acceptable manner. It is essential that the UK retains control over its interest rate, uses Bank of England intervention to smooth speculative fluctuations, encourages worldwide co-operation (through the G8) between central banks and aims for the maximum long-term exchange rate flexibility combined with the maximum practical short-term stability. Under such a regime, the exchange rate fulfils its role as facilitator of greater growth, higher living standards and full employment, without becoming an end in itself.

There is always a rate of exchange that enables each country to employ its productive resources fully. In an ever-changing environment, the rate frequently alters to secure simultaneous full employment and trade balance. Therefore, when formulating British economic policy outside the EU, any suggestion that the pound should 'shadow' the euro must be rebutted. Such targeting makes domestic objectives harder to achieve; in any case the pound moves more closely with the US dollar than with any European currency.

However, as the Chinese government has illustrated, it is possible for national governments to choose where they want the exchange rate to be and, over the long term, to hold it there within narrow margins. Of course there will be short-term fluctuations, but these are not important. It is the medium-term trend that counts. The question then becomes one of which policies can governments pursue to change the exchange rate, and then maintain it near the preferred level? A range of options is available which can be co-ordinated to generate a viable, nation-wide strategy.

Firstly, is the monetary and interest rate stance that the government adopts. Strong evidence exists that tight monetary policies and the high interest rates, which accompany them, pull the exchange rate up, while more accommodating monetary policies and lower interest rates bring it down. Secondly, the actions of both the government and the central bank, when dealing with the foreign exchange market, exert a powerful influence in an area where expectations are crucial. If the government expresses a clear view that the exchange rate is too high or too low, the market will respond. Thirdly, the government possesses a defined strategy to eliminate the foreign trade imbalance. Such a strategy requires a commitment to achieving a long-term competitive exchange rate, which achieves balance of payments equilibrium at full employment. This rate will, of course, alter over time. Fourthly, tariff protection may be crucial in order to restrict the flows of imports to a level consistent with the targeted short-term exchange rate. Fifth, on the capital side of the balance of payments the government can control international financial flows to maintain a competitive exchange rate. Potential policies range from taxes to quantitative restrictions on speculative movements.

However, if the value of the currency falls, there is a tendency for imports to stay initially at their previous volume, while the domestic revenue from exports falls because the exchange rate has gone down, the 'J curve' effect. A slow decline in the exchange rate generates a succession of such effects flowing from each successive decrease, giving the impression that no improvement is in sight. Nonetheless the empirical evidence of exchange rate movements occurring in Britain and other countries, and of the availability of a battery of policy instruments to sustain a targeted external currency value, demonstrates that in the medium-term governments can determine exchange rates.

Britain's exchange rate policy has lurched from the ultra fixed systems such as the Gold Standard, through Bretton Woods and the ERM, to the freely floating days when monetarism and the rule of markets swept through governments across the industrialised world.

Rarely has the decision to enter, or exit, one particular system been for any proven economic reasons. Instead the main driving force is whatever the current vogue of politicians and their advisers happen to be.

This is clearly an inefficient method of managing an economy, and of determining peoples' employment potential and standard of living. Rather within the context of this discussion concerning the development of an active exchange rate policy to facilitate national economic renewal, we argue that its over-riding function is to convert domestic prices of all factors of production, including, labour, energy, raw materials, into international prices at such a level as to encourage economic growth through the full use of resources and simultaneously to achieve trade balance. If the exchange rate cannot fulfil these functions over a sufficient period of time (to counter fluctuations), this offers conclusive evidence that the exchange rate is misaligned, so that the existing system must come under scrutiny.

An exchange rate system to suit all economies for all seasons is an impossible reality given the complexity of determining the exact exchange rate regime for a country in light of the arguments concerning flexible and fixed exchange rates (Baimbridge and Whyman, 2008). Two systems, however, offer the greatest potential for combining an exchange rate that secures balance of payments equilibrium with full employment.

Firstly, managed floating does not involve parities that the government is obliged to preserve. Instead the currency is free to float, but the authorities intervene to avoid what they regard to be undesirable consequences of excessive appreciation or depreciation. A weak currency may lead to excessive depreciation that the government may wish to avoid because of its repercussions on the domestic price of imports and the internal cost structure. Alternatively, countries with a strong currency may seek to avoid appreciation if they want to accumulate reserves and are indifferent to the effect on the money supply. Moreover, a country may even attempt to engineer the depreciation of its currency that would otherwise appreciate if the foreign exchange market were left to operate freely.

Secondly, multiple exchange rates offer a system whereby different exchange rates are enforced for different transactions either on the current or capital account. The IMF's official definition of a multiple exchange rate is 'an effective buying or selling rate which, as a result of official action, differs from parity by more than 1 per cent'. Multiple exchange rates can be viewed both as a form of exchange control (particularly over capital transactions) and as a rational response to the fact that different classes of goods have different price elasticities in world trade. Many countries, including Britain in the past with the 'dollar premium', charge a higher domestic price for foreign currency than the prevailing market rate for investment abroad in capital assets such as shares and property. Such a device acts in essence as a form of exchange control.

Misplaced criticism

Supporters of continued EU membership argue that the degree of economic autonomy for the nation state outlined here is illusory, because globalisation and the integration of financial markets will not allow differences in economic policy to persist. Therefore the UK might as well join the single currency. Indeed, many left-of-centre supporters of economic and monetary integration profess the belief that only as part of a new eurozone can governments become sufficiently powerful to operate a form of euro-Keynesianism without financial markets causing terminal destabilisation via a currency crisis. However, both viewpoints are over-stated. For example, the experience of the UK economy between 1990 and 1992 demonstrated that being tied into a fixed exchange rate system at an uncompetitively high rate leads to a fall in output and a rise in unemployment. However, departure from the ERM and the subsequent 20 per cent depreciation in sterling resulted in the resumption of economic growth, which facilitated a fall in unemployment to levels last experienced two-and-a-half decades earlier. Thus arguments that economic policy autonomy is impossible because of financial market integration are wrong, because both the UK's strategy and performance were significantly different from all other EU member states during this period; that is why it was so comparatively successful. Devaluation gave UK firms a much needed increase in competitiveness, which was not instantly lost due to inflation, as new classical theorists claim, but instead provided government with a freedom of manoeuvre that could have resulted in the adoption of either strategy outlined in this chapter or a multiplicity of alternatives.

A second argument for maintaining EU membership is the suggestion that the UK's European partners would engage in some form of trade protection, which would deny British firms access to the single internal market and therefore cause considerable damage to its economy should the UK remain outside the euro on a long-term basis. The argument is implausible. Firstly, the UK has suffered a substantial trade deficit with the rest of the EU since accession in 1973; therefore, in the event of a trade war, our EU 'partners' would lose the most. Secondly, any such protectionist measures would fall foul of the Treaty of Rome, the Single European Act, the TEU and the World Trade Organisation's regulations. All are international treaties, binding their signatories to respect reciprocity of trade.

Another argument favouring continued EU membership is that it will provide the UK with additional political influence over the future development of the EU. Independence, according to the argument, equals powerlessness. However, the claim is spurious. Whilst the participants in the single currency may opt to discuss their common economic policy apart from other EU member states, there is no legal mechanism for any other decisions to be taken in this way. Thus the UK cannot be marginalised simply due to its non-participation in the single currency. Moreover, its position would be strengthened further by consultation and co-operation with other EU member states who have exercised their opt-out (Denmark and Sweden) or been deemed too divergent for immediate membership (Greece). Further enlargement of the EU will increase the number of member countries incapable or unwilling to sacrifice other policy objectives for conformity to EMU's 'one size fits all' policies. When such uniform monetary measures create areas of high structural unemployment, as they inevitably will, it is essential for opt-out nations to possess a collectively pre-agreed strategy of vetoing any plan to provide EU-wide aid to those areas. Problems created by the euro's operations should not be the responsibility of non-participants, but should be wholly financed by those embracing the single currency. Additionally, because *all* historical monetary unions not based upon political union have collapsed amidst substantial economic difficulties, these non-members would be wise to encourage the EU to formulate a contingency plan for the re-establishment of individual currencies if (or when) the demise of the euro occurs.

In reality, Britain enjoys an effective long-run choice concerning its future strategy; it can embrace an essentially European identity or, if it decides to opt-out of the euro, it can pursue a global strategy. Moreover, the advantages of free trade within the EU and the imposition of a common external tariff on outside imports have become progressively smaller since 1973, as restrictions on trade have been steadily diminished worldwide. Under the auspices of GATT and its successor, the WTO, the average tariff on industrial goods between developed countries has been reduced to just 3.8 per cent. Consequently, the industrialised nations are closer to the free trade ideal than they have ever been. In this gradually emerging new world economy, access to the EU single internal market for UK business is assured.

Britain need not fear that a long-term disengagement with movements towards further EU integration will lead to a powerless isolation. Britain is a member of the 'G8' industrial nations; its economy ranks as one of the largest in the world and the third largest in the EU. It is a member of the World Bank and the International Monetary Fund. It possesses a seat on the United Nations Security Council and remains the head of the Commonwealth, whose potential for expanded trade has recently been grossly neglected (West, 1995; Burkitt *et al.*, 1996). Moreover, Britain enjoys a substantial portfolio of overseas assets and investments, and attracts the highest level of inward investment in the EU. It is the world's second largest financial centre and global investor. It has more companies in the world's top 500 than any other EU country. The UK is well placed to be one of the most dynamic and innovative global economies (Taylor, 1995).

Among Britain's greatest assets, underpinning its global economic effectiveness is the English language. More than 1,400 million people live in officially English-speaking countries. One in five of the world's population speaks English. By next year, more than a billion will be learning it. It is the main language of books, newspapers, international business, academic conferences, science, technology, diplomacy and the Internet. Of all electronically stored information, 80 per cent is in English.

The widely held view that Britain has 'no alternative' but to participate in European integration is at odds with the facts; instead a range of possible alternatives exists. Britain could remain an EU member and secure, under WTO rules, freely trading with the EMU-zone through a series of mutually beneficial, bilateral agreements. Alternatively, it could explore the possibility of a closer relationship with the North American Free Trade Association, whilst above all, it should intensify its trading and investment links with the Commonwealth and the nations of the Pacific Rim. In these ways Britain would be able to pursue its true contemporary role of global trader and investor, while at the same time retaining its scope for a largely autonomous economic and social policy, such as the two possible strategies detailed above. Furthermore, outside the single currency, the choice between and among such strategies would be taken through the democratic process.

Conclusion

The design of a macroeconomic framework for a complex advanced economy depends upon a multiplicity of diverse factors, including recognition of its unique industrial structure, monetary and fiscal policy transmission mechanisms, the practice of wage formation, propensity for owner-occupation, national savings rates and technological progress. A combination of differences in consumer tastes, political choices, natural resources and centres of competitive excellence, together with the actions of institutions established to implement economic and social policy, necessitates differences in economic policy between nations. Moreover, exchange rate regimes tend to have a greater impact upon smaller, export-orientated nations than upon their larger neighbours, where only a relatively small proportion of GDP is traded. Consequently, it is extremely difficult for one international economic authority to replace national macroeconomic management by one common interest or exchange rate. It is simply that many economies of EU member states are too divergent cyclically and structurally from their neighbours for any claim of prior convergence to be convincing and, without such evidence; a common economic strategy is unlikely to be simultaneously in their individual interests.

In view of such fundamental weakness at the heart of the EU project, the decision to reject participation retains for national government the economic instruments vital to successful macroeconomic management. Exchange rates can fulfil their function of equalising the demand and supply for a currency by the variation of its price, thereby preventing a basic uncompetitive imbalance from causing mass unemployment and falling standards of living. Fiscal policy, freed from the twin restrictions of the TEU convergence criteria and the Stability and Growth Pact, can smooth cyclical fluctuations, avoiding periodic unemployment that wastes productive resources and generates associated human misery. The purpose of monetary policy is, then, to prevent unstable boom and slump conditions in housing and financial markets, whilst seeking to ensure a low interest rate for investors in productive capital. Supply-side policies, including selective labour market programmes and investment in the economy's physical and IT superstructure, do not require a rejection of the single currency to be applied, although the benefit of a macroeconomic structure tailored to the needs of the economy would provide a more fertile environment for their implementation. Thus, rather than being weakened by the refusal to be dominated by an EU agenda, which will often conflict with the interests of its economy, the UK would be both stronger and possess a superior ability to adapt to changing international market conditions. In the process, democratic choice would be enhanced and encourage the UK to end its undue preoccupation with events in a small corner of the European continent at the expense of a vigorous attempt to meet the growing demands of emergent markets across the globe.

In view of the overwhelming evidence supporting the maintenance of national self-determination of economic policy, two factors remain to provide the momentum towards further integrationalist economic participation. The first relates to the determination of a small political elite, together with the representatives of multinational corporations, to complete the European integration project; the former perhaps seek the increased influence a 'United States of Europe' would play in world events, whereas the latter desire to evade national regulatory regimes and thereby enhance profits. However, these small elites are neither representative of the wider British electorate, nor even of the majority of business. In a democracy, governments should act in the interests of all the people, which requires the rejection of abandoning national economic policy.

The second factor undermining the vigorous assertion of national independence is the fear of failure. The notion of the UK as a declining nation has long sapped its resolve to follow its own interests and has caused many to prefer safety in 'Fortress Europe', with economic policy dictated by outside 'experts'. Yet, as illustrated in this chapter, there is no reason for such defeatism. Fear is the enemy of innovation and as the one of the largest economies in the world, the UK possesses a significant number of advantages. The question remains whether these can be better realised within an EU model of deeper economic and political integration, a looser relationship with the EU, or through a more independent arrangement, possibly involving withdrawal as a first step towards this reorientation of priorities. This is a question for considered evaluation of all the evidence and not to be closed off due to political prejudice or an ill thought through agenda that conflicts with contemporary debate. This is an important question since it goes to the very heart of what Britain will make of itself and whether it places artificial limitations upon its ability to deliver the priorities espoused by its citizens.

Notes

[1] Kydland and Prescott (1977) argue that rules or pre-commitment are more relevant when the monetary and fiscal authorities enjoy a

reputation for discipline and consistency over time, whereas discretionary policy is more appropriate when such credibility is lacking.

[2] It is worth noting that the international price structures of many of these key products are denominated in US dollars. Moreover, the euro is likely to have a more volatile medium-term relationship with the US dollar than sterling has experienced since the UK's withdrawal from the ERM in September 1992.

[3] The converse occasionally occurs, if import and export volumes do not change sufficiently to offset the price movements; the Marshall-Lerner condition states that the trade balance will improve when the sum of the elasticities of demand for exports and imports exceeds unity.

CHAPTER 9

A NEW SOCIAL POLICY FRAMEWORK

Introduction

One distinctive feature of the model of regional integration advanced by the EU concerns the creation of a social dimension (*espace social européen*), intended to counter-balance the less desirable consequences likely to arise from the unfettered operation of free market forces (Bean *et al.*, 1998). The concept of a 'social Europe' is typically counterpoised by the neo-liberal, free market 'Anglo-Saxon' model, and consequently has proven particularly popular amongst social democratic and trade union constituencies. Indeed, it represents a significant reason why these groupings remain amongst the most enthusiastic advocates of deeper European integration (Strange, 1997; Whyman, 2002; Baimbridge and Whyman, 2008).

Whilst attractive to this constituency as an alternative to an unrestrained, market-orientated 'American' model, however, the preferred European Social Model (ESM) is typically presented with little consideration of its plausibility and internal coherence. It is simply stated that deeper integration will result in an ESM, irrespective of whether the available evidence supports this point of view or not. There is little critical analysis exploring whether the creation and maintenance of an ESM is consistent with other elements of the European project, such as the form of EMU chosen as the key feature of the economic evolution of the Union, nor whether enlargement of the EU has further undermined the original conception of a social Europe. This chapter seeks to explore these questions. As a result, it does not examine questions relating to the cost of social regulations designed in Brussels, as this has been examined elsewhere (Minford *et al.*, 2005). Instead, the chapter concentrates upon the potential for the establishment of a successful ESM, and whether this endeavour contradicts and conflicts with the broader drift of European integration.

ESM: a definition

Despite its centrality as a feature of debate relating to the future development of the 'new Europe', it is perhaps surprising that the ESM remains poorly defined, including by the EU itself (Vaughan-Whitehead, 2003). One of the few attempts, arising from the Nice summit in 2000, suggested that the ESM derived from a 'common core of values' relating to the provision of a high degree of social protection, the recognition of the importance of dialogue between social partners and the necessity to promote social cohesion as essential elements within the process of European integration (EU, 2000:4). It is therefore intended to be more than the sum of the approximately 70 directives or legislative tools that seek to influence European social policy, principally in the fields of labour law, equal opportunities within the workplace, occupational health and safety and the free movement of labour.

In one sense, this is not surprising, because the social dimension has been grafted on to a framework established by the inaugural Treaty of Rome, concentrating upon the removal of trade barriers and the promotion of economic integration. Indeed, it was only during the Delors presidency of the European Commission that a Social Chapter was developed (in 1989) to advocate the creation of a minimum set of social rights for EU citizens. However, this remained a non-binding, political declaration, signed by 11 of the then 12 EU member states (the UK being the exception) until its evolution into a social protocol annexed to the Treaty on European Union (TEU) in 1992 whereby Article Two committed the EU:

> ... to promote economic and social progress and a high level of employment and to achieve balanced and sustainable development, in particular through the creation of an area without internal frontiers, through the strengthening of economic and social cohesion and through the establishment of economic and monetary union, ultimately including a single currency in accordance with the provisions of this Treaty. (EU Commission, 1992)

This was further strengthened by incorporating the protocol into the main body of the subsequent Amsterdam Treaty. The resulting Article 11 provided the EU Commission with new competences in the areas of industrial relations and combating social exclusion.

The ESM is, in essence, a variant of the post-war German *social market*, which has combined a successful, competitive market economy with generous welfare provision, labour protection and an exceptional vocational training system that produced skilled workers of sufficient quantity and quality, thereby rectifying the corporate tendency to under-invest in skill formation (Teague, 1997). It is a multi-faceted approach encompassing elements of economic, social and labour market policy, including:

- Competitive market economy, but where social institutions mediate between state and market. In the original conception, the ESM has been associated with the prioritisation of full employment, through euro-Keynesianism, as advocated by the Tindemans (1976) report prepared for the EU Commission, but more recently this element has been downgraded, for example through the Lisbon agenda.

- Promoting social solidarity, primarily through initiatives designed to reduce inequality and protect worker–citizen rights. In social policy terms, this embraces support for the extension of universal, comprehensive welfare state provision to cover all EU citizens, and thereby create a minimum safety net for European citizens across the entire Single Internal Market, seeking to reduce inequality and enhance social cohesion. It also includes universal employee protection whilst at work.

- Combining the desirability of universality (through social protocols) with the realisation of the subsidiarity principle through encouraging social partners to complement state activity. The promotion of 'voice' rather than 'exit' includes social partnership between employers and employees, typically, though not exclusively, through trade unions.

There are areas of dispute relating to the conception of the ESM, not least between trade unions and employer organisations over the pressure exerted by the former to broaden collective bargaining across member states rather than remaining a predominantly national preserve (so-called euro-bargaining).

A coherent model?

The discussion of the ESM, thus far, suggests that it is a well considered, internally consistent entity, fully realised in practice across the internal market created by all established EU member states. However, this is far from the case. There is considerable divergence between the social and employment policies pursued by individual nations, with the Scandinavian and UK Anglo-Saxon models representing two extremes. Moreover, the current form of social dimension being constructed across the EU is a minimalist version of a fully-fledged system of social protection of the idealised version outlined, above (see Table 9.1).

Table 9.1 Comparison of ideal social market and current EU 'social dimension'

	EU social dimension	Ideal European social market
Welfare State		
Type	Minimalist	Comprehensive
Coverage	Safety net	Universal
Replacement ratio	Low	High
Association with labour market	Re-commodification	De-commodification
Response to globalisation	Competitive – improve labour market skills	Protective – social citizenship requires non-market income source to make effective choices
Industrial relations		
Collective bargaining recognition	Patchy	High/Comprehensive
Corporatist	Diverse – some member states deregulated wage formation, whilst others rely upon social contracts to secure budget cuts	Established – facilitates superior inflation: employment trade-off
Euro-level IR	Minimum – EWC, consultation only	Developed – framework bargaining between federal-level social partners
Labour regulation	Minimum – complements single market; over-regulation impedes competitiveness	Fundamental – basis of social accord, combining industrial adjustment with employee protection

Conflict between EMU and ESM?

The economy

The ultimate viability of the ESM depends upon the economic success of the European economy, both in terms of this generating the resources necessary to finance social measures and generous forms of labour market protection, but also because economic failure would place a considerable strain upon social interventions intended to mollify negative consequences. The predictable impact of a nation state joining EMU is understandably uncertain because monetary union of this type has no historical precedent (Goodhart, 1995). Supporters of the process claim that the combination of greater exchange rate stability, reduced transaction costs, enhanced competition deriving from price transparency and low real interest rates resulting from a successful ECB anti-inflation strategy, will provide a virtuous cycle of increased business confidence, trade, investment and growth. Opponents of this process, however, argue that the loss of monetary and exchange rate policy instruments is likely to increase instability amongst countries which are incompletely converged. They will be therefore more likely to suffer from asymmetric external shocks which the ECB will be incapable of moderating by use of its only policy instrument; interest rates. Furthermore, the ECB may itself become a second source of instability if it seeks to establish anti-inflation credibility with the financial markets by over-tightening monetary policy and thereby increasing unemployment. These issues are discussed in more detail in Chapter 8, yet the conclusions arising from this debate have critical importance for the potential sustainability of the ESM.

A second related question relates to the extent to which the economic framework, even if successful in general macroeconomic terms, might work against the grain of the proposed ESM. There are a number of potential points of concern in this regard. The TEU, establishing the particular version of EMU adopted by the EU, is inherently deflationary due to its restrictions placed upon autonomous government policy. It states that budget deficits and national debt must not be 'excessive', defined, by Article 104c(2) of the Treaty, as where deficits exceeded 3 per cent of GDP for reasons other than those of a temporary or exceptional nature and where debt exceeds 60 per cent of GDP and is not declining at a 'satisfactory' pace (EU Commission, 1992).

The consequence of these rules has been member states reducing public expenditure and instituting public sector wage restraint in order to qualify for EMU membership, thereby depressing European growth rates for a decade and exacerbating already high levels of unemployment (Holland, 1995). Repercussions have included a series of strikes and demonstrations across Europe, protesting about cuts in public services and pay restraint, together with the first signs of severe recruitment problems in many public sector occupations. In some countries, including Italy and Portugal, corporatist agreements have been reached with trade union movements to reduce pensions and deregulate labour markets, with the unions receiving nothing in return except a promise to *reduce* the social wage in order to meet the Maastricht Convergence Criteria (Teague, 1998).

The commitment to fiscal policy restrictions does not, however, end once a country is accepted for participation in EMU, because the Growth and Stability Pact (GSP) threatens to fine member states who fail to comply with the 3 per cent deficit limit without their economies suffering severe recession. Exceptional circumstances are defined as national income declining by 0.75 per cent in a given year. However, since budget balances vary by perhaps 10 per cent over a trade cycle, compliance with the GSP may require surpluses of 7 per cent of GDP in years of healthy economic growth, representing an unprecedented tightening of public finances in a short period of time, and due to no obvious economic rationale. This would necessitate large cuts in public expenditure and a further decade of slow growth in Europe. Furthermore, the environment would hardly appear conducive to the development of euro-Keynesian policies aimed at reducing unemployment. Indeed, the GSP would effectively prevent the counter-cyclical fiscal policy, which would form a central feature of such a strategy. Thus, the macroeconomic features of a social democratic ESM conflict with the requirements of the Maastricht version of EMU.

Partnership at work?

The labour market will become an increasingly important source of economic stability (or instability) once a nation state participates in monetary union. Indeed, this forms one of Gordon Brown's 'Five Tests' when assessing the potential consequences of UK participation in EMU (HM Treasury, 1997). As alternative instruments previously used to adjust the competitiveness of an industry (or economy) are no longer available, member states will depend upon the ability of wage formation systems to deliver wages consistent with international competitiveness. This requires aggregate wages to grow in line with productivity. Studies indicate that this may be best achieved through co-ordinated wage bargaining, occurring at central or industrial level, where all parties can internalise the inflationary implications of their decisions (Bruno and Sachs, 1985; Calmfors and Driffill, 1988; Amoroso and Jespersen, 1992). Hence, the Netherlands, Germany and Ireland have followed this strategy during their transition to EMU (Teague, 1998).

This strategy, however, encounters two problems. Firstly, for voluntary organisations like trade unions to accept lower wages than a free market may allow, they require compensation of a form that their members will accept as justification for their stance, or haemorrhage members and influence. A typical demand is for a degree of wage equalisation to be included in wage formation, thereby narrowing differentials. Secondly, co-ordinated wage bargaining is less able to incorporate micro-flexibility demanded by corporations more interested in utilising wages to devise incentives for employees to increase productivity whilst responding to diverse patterns of industrial change (Marsden, 1992). However, decentralisation of industrial relations systems threatens destabilising competition between unions, and/or the sidelining of collective bargaining (Pissarides, 1997).

Failure to ensure that wages grow in line with productivity, perhaps due to demands for equalisation of pay emanating from wage transparency due to a single currency, can have devastating results. The reunification of East and West Germany in 1989 occurred at parity exchange rates, together with pressure from unions and political parties for wage equalisation intended to indicate universal citizenship and prevent mass labour migration to the West, despite the former economy being only half as productive. Predictably, output declined by 67% in the first year after unification, leading to 25 per cent of the entire labour market losing their jobs (Buechtemann and Schupp, 1992). This was despite official transfers to East Germany averaging DM 140bn per annum (i.e. 4–5 per cent of GDP), between 1991 and 1997, with an equivalent additional sum transferred from local government, pensions and other public funds (Flockton, 1998). Thus, German reunification provides stark warning of the dangers of mishandling a rapid transition towards EMU when currencies are overvalued, economies incompletely converged and pressures for wage equalisation exacerbate stagflationary pressures (Horn and Zwiener, 1992).

Social partnership offered by an ESM has a far greater potential than concerning the macroeconomic impact of wage formation alone, but legitimises collective bargaining as the primary focus for reaching industrial consensus. An embryo system of euro-bargaining could be stimulated by EU initiatives such as the EWC Directive. Alternatively,

TNCs may substitute increased concentration upon internal labour markets irrespective of national borders to the stabilisation of national labour markets, thereby tailoring working conditions to their particular perception of changing patterns of demand resulting from the intensification of international competition. Advances in information technology have facilitated a shift from administrative to performance-based control, with responsibility and accountability devolved to business units at lower levels of large organisations (Sisson and Marginson, 1995).

The former may, indeed, strengthen consultation between management and national unions representing workers in individual member states and potentially establish a form of 'arms length' pattern bargaining to establish universal minimum standards of training, anti-discrimination practice and promotion procedures (Rhodes, 1992). However, multi-employer bargaining is, however, ill suited to systems of 'managed autonomy', where central management maintains control through a range of performance measures and incentives (Marginson and Sisson, 1996:177–8). Indeed, this process may result in trade union marginalisation due to employer preference for company-level productivity coalitions rather than coordinated bargaining at central or sectoral level (Windolf, 1989).

It is, furthermore, possible that the creation of a harmonised European labour market may be limited to certain key groups of workers, possessing specific technical and managerial skills, and for particular categories of highly mobile labour, notably managers, construction workers, labourers and young people (Walsh *et al.*, 1995). The creation of a duality of labour markets split between core and periphery workers would undermine national labour market cohesion, as wage differentials efficient for the organisation may fuel demands for comparable incomes from workers in similar occupations. Trade unions would face fragmentation along supranational company lines or abandon efforts to stabilise national labour markets and become 'partners ... of regional capital trying to survive in inter-regional free market competition' (Streeck and Schmitter, 1991:55). Thus, according to this viewpoint, euro-bargaining is irrelevant to the needs of post-Fordist flexible production (Rhodes, 1992).

Divergent influences upon industrial relations systems are likely to persist into EMU, with certain labour market institutions likely to prove superior in maintaining existing arrangements to others. Hence, the most likely prediction is for an uneven and spasmodic development of industrial relations, with the eventual emergence of an ad hoc, partly institutionalised system of pan-European labour relations (Rhodes,

1992). Nevertheless, irrespective of the eventual evolution of industrial relations throughout Europe, social partners face increasing challenges resulting from the changing composition of the European labour market and the tensions between corporate demands for greater micro- and macro-flexibility. Thus, the regulatory framework inherent within an ESM is likely to conflict with fundamental requirements emanating from EMU, together with certain corporate reactions to increased international competitive pressure, itself exacerbated by price transparency due to a single currency.

Social citizenship and the ESM

The final element involved in constructing an ESM concerns the combination of European social policy and labour regulation, which the EU Commission promotes as being sufficient to counterbalance excessive pressures on employees emanating from a combination of the single market and EMU. Current measures, encapsulated in the Social Chapter, have ensured a degree of protection for employees in cases of collective redundancies, restrictions on working hours, the establishment of European Works Councils, minimum maternity rights, enhanced health and safety protection and equal treatment for workers on irregular contracts. These measures have delivered a number of real benefits to workers in lightly regulated economies such as the UK. However, whilst unfair to dismiss such achievements as meaningless, nor wishing to treat the social dimension as though it were a complete and coherent approach, it is nevertheless grossly insufficient for the EU Commission to portray this as a distinct ESM.

The high fragmentation of social policy within, and between, EU member states implies that European regulation is only possible for non-contentious issues, where nations share common interests and goals, such as health and safety matters. Otherwise, social protection will occur only at the lowest common denominator (Keller and Sorries, 1997). Barnard and Deakin (1997:131) criticise the current approach as nothing more than an 'eclectic body of employment law', whilst others claim the approach has a 'hollow core' (Leibfried, 1994:246; Leibfried and Pierson, 1995). Thus, the presentation of the EU's social dimension as the basis for a social citizenship is premature, as the existing minimalist safety-net framework has little measurable impact outside member states with particularly weak regulation. Moreover, Streeck (1992:218–19) argues that the 'retarded advancement of European-level political rights' and the 'almost complete absence of an European system of industrial citizenship' indicate that there is little reason to anticipate these initiatives proving particularly successful.

Consequently, it is a moot point whether the subsidiarity principle informs and reinforces the considerable fragmentation in this area of policy, or is actually an *ex post facto* attempt to recognise and provide a narrative to justify the divergence in social and employment matters across the EU member states.

It is possible to criticise this rather negative conclusion by suggesting that gaps in the EU social dimension will be progressively filled and it will ultimately evolve into a variant of an ESM. However, this ignores the increasingly vocal neo-liberal critique of welfare states, labour regulation and centralised wage bargaining as causes of 'Eurosclerosis' (Lawrence and Schultz, 1987). Generous welfare provision has been criticised by a number of economists as being responsible for a decline in economic performance (Feldstein, 1974, 1976; Lindbeck *et al*, 1994). Increases in taxation to fund higher levels of government transfers are suggested to reduce work incentives, increase the rate of natural unemployment and depress economic dynamism, whilst social security reduces personal savings rates, thereby reducing the stock of capital and hence national income. Job security legislation is claimed to produce hysteresis, where an individuals' duration of unemployment is negatively related to their probability of getting a job (Lawrence and Schultz, 1987). However, the evidence is mixed, with welfare expenditure acting as an automatic stabiliser to prevent a drift into recession, whilst social insurance may enable workers to take greater risks in their working lives which may produce greater returns for society as a whole (Korpi, 1996; Barr, 1992). Moreover, the corporatist combination of active labour market policies and co-ordinated wage formulation tend to improve the unemployment: inflation trade-off (Jackman *et al.*, 1990; Rhodes, 1992).

Nevertheless, the neo-liberal argument has been at least partially adopted by leading European politicians, as demonstrated by former British Prime Minister, Tony Blair, emphasising the need for all EU member economies to restructure their traditional approaches to social welfare and labour regulation. Indeed, in a speech, Blair pointedly rejected the 'old social model' in Europe, and argued that, 'our welfare systems and labour markets will require fundamental reform' (Blair, 2000). Additionally, in his introduction to the DTI White Paper *Fairness at Work*, Blair claimed that, even after adoption of the social chapter and minimum wage, the UK still has 'the most lightly regulated labour market of an leading economy in the world' (cited in Coates, 1999:653). Furthermore, these arguments are not restricted to the UK. In Germany, the costs of welfare provision, as non-wage labour costs, are seen as a prime factor contributing to the *Standortfrage*, namely questioning whether Germany has become wholly uncompetitive as a production location (Flockton, 1998). Moreover, the ECB's former senior economist, Otmar Issing, blamed the poor performance of the euro on 'the adverse impact of minimum wage and employment protection legislation', which can only be overcome by a 'comprehensive programme of structural reform' (cited in *The Guardian*, 13 May 2000, p.24).

In practice, this consists of creating what Cerny (1990) describes as a transition from welfare state to '*competition state*', in which policies are determined by the perceived demands of survival in the global economy. This requires the creation of flexible labour markets (on the microeconomic definition) and the promotion of industrial adjustment to global change. The competition state would re-commodify workers, replacing *protection from* globalised competition with the provision of education and training initiatives intended to *provide skills and resources to succeed* in this new competitive environment. The paradox is that many progressive supporters of further and deeper European integration take this stance at least in part because of their expectations of the successful development of an ESM, at the same time that many EU governments are increasingly questioning the future of this very model. Consequently, the ESM approach looks less viable as a future model for euro-land than in previous circumstances.

Enlargement and diversity

The impact of the 2004 and 2007 rounds of EU enlargement will have a significant impact upon the exacerbation of diversity, both in terms of the likely impact upon the new member states (NMS), the social provision and employment protection afforded by the EU(15) nations and the potential for the creation of a fully functioning ESM within the larger Europe:

- Wage levels: all but one (Cyprus) of the NMS have lower average annual gross earnings in industry and services than the EU(15) member states, with rates exceeding €40,000 in Denmark, Germany, Luxembourg and the UK, contrasting markedly with equivalent rates in Hungary (€7,100), Poland (€6200), Slovakia (€5700) and Latvia (€3,800) (Eurostat, 2005).

- Employment participation rates: once again, of the NMS, only Cyprus (67.9 per cent) supersedes the EU average (70.6 per cent), albeit that within the more established member states the Southern European states (in particular Italy) have much lower participation rates than this EU(15) average rate. Overall, the labour market participation rate for the NMS is only 56 per cent (EU Commission, 2006).

- Unemployment: the unemployment rate within the NMS, averaging 13.4 per cent, is substantially higher than the 7.9 per cent average for the EU(15), yet these figures conceal a wide variation, with unemployment rates of 6 per cent in Cyprus and Slovenia, whilst Slovakia had a jobless rate exceeding 16 per cent and Poland almost 18 per cent (EU Commission, 2006). Comparable figures for other EU countries range from the 4–5 per cent experienced by Denmark, Ireland, Luxembourg, the Netherlands, Austria and the UK, whilst rates peak at 9–10 per cent in Greece, Spain, France and Germany.

- Casualisation of work: many of the NMS economies have a marked divergence from EU(15) forms of labour market flexibility, with far higher rates of self-employment, as a means of evading national labour regulations, as opposed to a far higher incidence of temporary and part-time employment contracts amongst more established EU member states.

- Industrial relations: the majority of the NMS have comparatively weak central employer organisations and, with the exceptions of Slovenia, Cyprus and Malta, have relatively low and declining trade union membership rates (Vaughan-Whitehead, 2003). Moreover, with the dual exceptions of Slovenia and Slovakia, the dominant level of wage bargaining for the NMS is at company level, rather than the sectoral level more typical across the majority of the EU(15) member states; the UK is the most obvious exception to this trend, with its emphasis upon company-level wage setting.

- Distribution of income: the accession of the NMS has widened the existing income disparity *between* member states, with the GDP per capita (measured in PPS) of individual member states ranging from 40 per cent of the EU(15) average in Latvia, to 210 per cent in Luxembourg (EU Commission, 2006). Moreover, income inequality within individual nations, measured by the Gini coefficient, tends to be significantly higher within the NMS than EU(15) nations; the exception, once again, being the UK, which exhibits greater inequality than most new entrants (Vaughan-Whitehead, 2003).

Enlargement, therefore, has magnified a number of existing challenges inherent within the EU's stated objective of creating a meaningful and sustainable ESM. The diversity of experience between member states, in the areas of social policy and labour market regulation, has made it more difficult to establish a single approach to these issues across all member states. The resultant degree of fragmentation in social policy suggests that the establishment of a common European approach towards social protection might be restricted to a minimal safety net, or else focus upon less contentious issues (such as health and safety) where member states share a closer similarity of interests. Even this will prove difficult to achieve, since lower standards of regulation and welfare expenditure form central features of the strategies adopted by many of the NMS determined to maintain national competitiveness to facilitate the 'catch-up' development process, raising the GDP per capita from only half the EU(15) average figure (EU Commission, 2006).

The persistence of the diversity of social provision within the enlarged EU presents a particular problem for the development of the ESM, to the extent that the 'social gap' could prove to be a form of 'social dumping', whereby governments may maintain lower social and/or labour standards in order to gain a competitive advantage over another national economy. To the extent that this succeeds, it may pressurise other member states to recover their competitive position by weakening their own labour legislation and social provisions, resulting in 'beggar thy neighbour' strategies resulting in a 'race to the bottom'. This is precisely the type of behaviour that the ESM is supposed to inhibit. However, whilst it is certainly the case that both wage levels and social provision are significantly lower within the NMS than the EU(15) average, this only widens the already considerable differences between the more established member states.

One of the primary reasons for the lower wages and less developed social protection systems relates to the inferior productivity rates in the NMS; averaging only 58 per cent of the equivalent levels in the EU(15) nations (EU Commission, 2006). To attempt to equalise wages and/or social provision without an equivalent rise in total factor productivity would provide a severe shock to these economies and impose a weighty burden upon their fledgling development profiles or a similar type that devastated the former East German economy in the aftermath of the German reunification process (Buechtemann and Schupp, 1992). Consequently, the challenge for the EU, in the development of the ESM, is to distinguish between nation states weakening social protection measures in order to pursue what might be considered to be 'unfair competition', and where lower social standards relate to weaker economic fundamentals and might be considered appropriate to the individual country's particular stage of development (Leibfried and Pierson, 1994).

Prompting a strategic re-evaluation?

The conclusion reached by this chapter is that the perception of a fully developed ESM, operating comfortably within an EMU founded upon the rules and restrictions outlined in the TEU, is improbable. In many respects, the two approaches are contradictory in essence. Consequently, those supporters of further and deeper European integration should urgently re-evaluate their position to prevent cognitive dissonance—the holding of two contradictory ideas at the same time. There would appear to be three alternatives. The first is to dismiss the evidence contained in this chapter as unreliable, and to maintain the current stance. This enjoys the comfort, resulting from the maintenance of a constant and familiar position, even if it proves to be incorrect. However, there is a considerable amount of risk associated with this approach. If euro-land does, indeed, develop closer to the neo-liberal than ESM model of economy and society, this particular form of compromise is likely to satisfy neither social democrats nor conservatives, as the former will experience frustration that the full model of ESM has not been realised, whereas the latter will prove equally frustrated at the cost and perceived unnecessary constraint of market determination that even a minimalist version of social Europe would imply.

A second alternative would be for advocates of the creation of an ESM to pressurise the EU Commission to deliver on their promises, by making their continued support for the integration project conditional upon the successful completion of a progressive form of social Europe. This shift of approach is likely to result in intensive pressure being exerted in an attempt to cause a return to unconditional support, as this stance would undoubtedly weaken integration momentum, at least in the short run. Nevertheless, if support is to be used as a bargaining position to secure the ultimate achievement of a desired objective, then such pressure would have to be resisted. Moreover, to ensure that the conditionality is taken seriously, ESM supporters would be required to convince other political actors that they will indeed oppose future integration initiatives, if not support the re-nationalisation of certain policy areas. Successful negotiating theory suggests the necessity of a viable threat or negative consequence that is understood and believed by all parties if demands are to be taken seriously.

The only other alternative would be for advocates of a progressive social model to realise the internal inconsistencies lying at the heart of the European project, and prefer to focus upon the realisation of a national version of the fundamental features of the ESM. This would have the advantage of ensuring that the individual elements were designed with the individual nation state in mind, and avoid the problems that harmonisation were likely to involve. That is to say undermining competitive advantage in low-wage NMS and setting rates so low as to be of little consequence for more affluent nations.

CHAPTER 10

A NEW POLITICAL SOVEREIGNTY FRAMEWORK

Introduction

Politicians like to talk of Britain being (or seeking to be) 'at the heart of Europe' (Johnson, 2002:185). Yet, the implications of this ambition are quite profound and remain relatively undeveloped despite the periodic 'sound and fury' of public debate on the issue. Indeed, former Labour Party leader Gaitskell, famously claimed that EU membership would mean '... the end of Britain as an independent state ... the end of a thousand years of history' (Labour Party Conference Report, 1962:154–65).

The European project has profound implications for social, political and economic aspects of national life, as has been demonstrated in this volume. This is certainly the case in terms of the development of national, sovereign, democratic self-determination, as will be explored in this chapter. Yet, part of the problem in terms of public understanding of the consequences of European integration is that, when asked to approve this direction of travel back in 1975 in a national referendum on continued membership of what has evolved into the EU, the British people were asked to vote for a common market and not the wider European 'project' (Redwood, 2001:163).[1]

Repeated assurances were given by the Heath government that membership would involve no serious derogation from British parliamentary sovereignty (Johnson, 2002:190). For example, the Conservatives' 1971 White Paper, stressing the economic and political benefits of entry, dismissed the notion that entry would undermine national sovereignty, instead outlining 'a sharing and an enlargement of individual national sovereignties in the general interest' (HMG, 1971). Indeed, Heath consistently maintained that EU membership did not involve ceding sovereignty, but rather pooling it; not giving it away, but rather sharing it with other member states (Heath, 2000:205). However, this sits uncomfortably with the preamble to the European Coal and Steel Community (ECSC), ratified in 1951, which was quite explicit in its anticipated objectives, when it stated that it perceived the organisation as 'the first step to the federation of Europe' (Broad, 2001:25). Moreover, the Cabinet Office (1961) had recognised that EU membership would result in a 'gradual surrender of sovereignty' that would result in Britain 'committing itself to a range of indefinite obligations over a wide field of action within the economic and social sphere'. Similarly, Sir Roderick Barclay (1960), then Head of the British Delegation to the European Commission, warned that the objective of the EU was 'not merely harmonisation but the unification of policies in every field of the economic union, economic policy, social policy, commercial policy, tariff policy and fiscal policy.'

Reticence to discuss issues of sovereignty might derive from the observation that a majority of British citizens remain suspicious of the European 'project' and oppose the gradual erosion of their rights of self-government (Johnson, 2002:192). Nevertheless, it would appear reasonable to conclude that there has long been a 'clear tendency towards obfuscation, if not deceit' on behalf of the political class when discussing the implications for sovereignty and self-determination arising from UK participation in the EU (Mullen, 2010).

Sovereignty in theory

Sovereignty may be defined as the possession and exercise of 'absolute and unlimited power' (Heywood, 1999:90) such that there is usually a distinction made between legal and political sovereignty, in that the former holds that the ultimate and final authority derives from the law of the state, whereas the latter is concerned with the realised distribution of power (Heywood, 1999:91). Hence, British understanding of politics differs somewhat from continental norms in that there has been more emphasis placed upon government, functions and institutions rather than the state as a distinct legal entity with a sense of moral unity (Johnson, 2002:194).

Malcolm (1996:355) argues that state sovereignty derives from the acceptance by the political community, so that legal authority is validated by political authority, and where the rules for the exercise of that authority (or constitution) are independent of other states. This gives rise to ultimate political and legal authority, producing 'sovereign authority'. According to this definition, sovereignty cannot be divided into individual elements, even amongst horizontal lines as may be found in federal constitutions, because each regional assembly is not exercising its own mini-sovereignty but rather is being allowed to exercise at local level the sovereign authority of the federal state in specific areas. Sovereignty cannot be delegated, but the exercise of this authority can be delegated, granting limited and specific competence to perform specific tasks.

Developing this argument, therefore, sovereignty cannot be pooled, although this can occur with respect to political power. To this point, Britain has delegated the exercise of specific areas of sovereign authority to the EU, where it has a degree of representation. However, the delegations were made by treaty and statute, and these laws were expressions of national sovereign authority. Nevertheless, whilst the delegation of the exercise of authority does not, in itself, threaten sovereignty, it does undermine democratic self-government, and therefore weakens the acceptance and acquiescence of the citizenry upon which sovereign authority is founded. Moreover, the more areas delegated, the less like a sovereign state a nation would become, and the easier it would be to convert long-term delegations into a formal arrangement of sovereign dependency. For Malcolm (1996:361–2), therefore, the more authority is delegated, the more likely it is that a nation will ultimately lose its sovereignty in the long run.

In the 1975 referendum, there was considerable discussion of the concept of 'pooled' sovereignty, namely where a number of individual member states might gain greater influence over their own economies by acting in concert, even though they have to surrender their monopoly over decision-making in the process. Thus, small nations may gain greater influence over their external economic and political environment through group action, even where this may result in a form of compromise that does not deliver to each nation everything that it would wish. Critics of this concept argued that it was not convincing because people either have the right to govern themselves subject to constraints outside their control, or this right is transferred, in whole or in part, to supra-national bodies. Hence, there is no intermediate point in between these alternatives. This point at least seems to have been conceded by supporters of continued EU membership, such as former Labour Party Deputy Leader, Roy Hattersley, who, writing 25 years after the referendum, questioned whether the pro-EU campaign had been straightforward on the sovereignty issue. For Hattersley: 'Joining the European Community involved loss of significant sovereignty, but by telling the British people that was not involved, I think the...argument was prejudiced for the next 30 years.' (Cited in Broad, 2001:108).

Supremacy of law: national or European?

In a parliamentary democracy, the supreme power rests in the sovereignty of the people, temporarily ceded to their elected parliamentary representatives and used to create legislation that has pre-eminence over all other rules created by other nations outside this national territory. Thus, the British (unwritten) constitution is based upon two main propositions, namely parliamentary sovereignty, where Acts of Parliament are always the supreme source of authority, and that a parliament cannot bind its successors (Redwood, 1997:201–02).

EU membership, however, posed significant changes in a number of respects, including the assertion that EU law took precedence over British law. One powerful example of this concerned the *aquis communitaire,* which refers to the process whereby all new entrants to the EU must accept all existing laws, rules and regulations without having the ability to question or renegotiate anything in the national interest. Moreover, this European Court has ruled that, when the EU has laid down rules for the implementation of a common policy, EU institutions have exclusive competence to enter into agreements with non-member states that affect these rules.

The legal basis for the supremacy of EU law over national law derives from a decision taken by the European Court of Justice (ECJ), in 1964, in effect, declaring its own supreme legal authority across the EU, as it has gradually shifted from adjudicating cases to interpreting and making law (Redwood, 1997:202). Thus, the House of Lords is no longer the supreme court in the land, but must refer questions of EU law to the European Court and be bound by its rulings. It is, moreover, the duty of national governments to implement EU laws within their territory. Hence, EU regulations impose quotas upon UK fishermen exercising their trade in UK territorial waters and a nation would violate Article 5 of the Treaty of Rome if it attempted to enter into any international treaty conflicting with EU law. Furthermore, EU competence even extends to the ability to raise taxation and spend monies within each member state independently of the government's overall macroeconomic policy stance. Certainly, this provoked the then leader of the Labour Party opposition, Harold Wilson, in a speech given to the Parliamentary Press Gallery, on 30 January 1973, to claim that:

> In 93 legislative words, the safeguards gained after centuries of constitutional struggle, and even bloody civil wars, were swept aside by a provision that said simply that hereafter anything enacted by the EEC automatically becomes a British law, annulling any laws which were inconsistent without debate. We have been sold, with hardly a murmur from the media, our constitutional birthright for a mess of highly problematical economic pottage. (Burkitt, 1975:8)

The assertion, made by the ECJ, that it cannot be challenged by national legal order, presents a direct challenge to sovereign authority, as it suggests that, were the British parliament ever to pass a statute repealing its accession legislation and/or varying its delegations granted to the EU, the ECJ could over-rule this decision (Malcolm, 1996:362). Whether this possibility would be realisable in practice is an open question, however, as it would depend upon the balance of political opinion and institutional resources available to assert European over national authority. This essentially repeats Malcolm's point, that sovereignty ultimately derives its strength from the acceptance of its validity by the relevant citizenry, and in its absence, can only be maintained by coercion. It is unlikely that the ECJ could or would seek to adopt this degree of confrontation in the face of a determined national government complete with an unambiguous democratic mandate on the issue.

Sovereignty in use

The theoretical definition of sovereignty, as expressed above, relates to the ultimate authority of the law of the state, independent from determination by other sources of legal authority. Essentially, sovereignty is related to a nation's supremacy within its own territorial boundaries. In the British case, that law made by the British parliament retains precedence, and all other aspects are delegated for exercise by other agencies by the will of the British parliament. Thus, what one government and what one act of legislation can create, another can amend or repeal. To the extent that this pertains, British sovereignty remains intact. However, widening the discussion slightly from the legal basis of sovereign authority towards its use, then the debate becomes more complicated.

It would be a reasonable assumption to make to assume that most people view sovereignty as a means to an end. Thus, for it to be more than simply a theoretical construct, it has to be realised in practice. In these terms, sovereignty *in use* relates to the pre-eminence of national decision-making and the independence of the nation state to pursue its own distinctive agenda. This is not to suggest that sovereignty is necessarily absolute in the sense that no external factors impinge upon freedom of action. Global markets, the actions of trans-national corporations and agreements reached through international treaties all constrain national action to a certain degree. However, it is the degree of independent autonomy that a nation possesses, when it chooses to respond to such external stimuli, that this section concerns.

Democracy

The UK system of parliamentary democracy rests upon the concept of the sovereignty of the people. Through their exercise of the franchise, they lend their sovereign power to elected representatives to exercise on their behalf for the limited duration of a single parliament. Membership of the EU may, therefore, weaken the British representative system of democracy by transferring control over a sizeable section of public life to the EU Commission and the Council of Ministers, which are distanced from being elected or dismissed by the British electorate (Burkitt, 1975:5). The democratic deficit has been mollified, to a degree, by the introduction of the European Parliament, through which the British electorate have an input, however, although this institution is gradually expanding its influence in holding the EU Commission to account and potentially influencing the development of directives, accountability and democratic determination is imperfect and imprecise. The EU organisational infrastructure represents a hybrid of federal and intergovernmental forms that aim to elevate power and decision-making divorced from the citizenry, thus insulating the EU from democracy and weakening the effective channels of communication between citizens and their government upon which the maintenance of individual liberties depends.

British membership of the EU involves a significant transfer of powers from the legislature to the executive, even on those areas where Britain retains a degree of control. The British executive determines the degree of parliamentary scrutiny that takes place relating to EU regulation and legislation, whilst the secrecy surrounding Council of Ministers meetings hampers the accountability of individual ministers for their decisions to parliament and hence the British people. Parliamentary democracy establishes the right of electors to elect and dismiss MPs and, thereby, governments, thereby enshrining accountability. EU institutions are not equally accountable. Indeed, no commissioners, and only one member of the Council of Ministers, can be elected and dismissed by the British people, and then only indirectly.

One important safeguard for the protection of individual liberties arises from the separation of executive, legislative and judicial functions. The EU violates this principle because the EU Commission possesses an element of initiative in each of the three areas. Furthermore, EU membership imposes constraints and duties upon these individuals which do not derive from UK legislation, and thereby in discharging their duties, government ministers and civil servants are not accountable to parliament and nor to the British people. Members of the British parliament can vote to change any law or tax on a majority vote, yet EU regulations and directives cannot be repealed or altered by the UK parliament. The British law courts are intended to uphold and enforce all legislation passed by parliament, until such a time as parliament repeals or changes it. EU membership, by contrast, requires UK courts to uphold and enforce EU laws that have not been passed nor scrutinised, amended or repealed, by the British parliament. Furthermore, Clause 2:4 of the EC Act stipulated that EU regulations and treaty articles prevail over Acts of Parliament—thus giving EU law precedence in the even of any conflict with UK law

Finally, the enshrinement of the free movement of labour and capital, within the Treaty of Rome, effectively prevents British citizens deciding to extend the scope of democratic influence into the economic sphere, and thereby facilitating macroeconomic and industrial relations policy. The creation of a single internal market further erodes the power of a nation state to pursue certain social and economic programmes, even if these had been explicitly endorsed by majority democratic opinion. Thus, EU membership arguably conflicts with democratic policy self-determination.

Economic sovereignty

An additional element encompassed within the concept of national sovereignty refers to the ability of a nation state to create sufficient political and economic space to be able to create a different type of society than other leading world economies. In this regard, it has been suggested that, by joining together, medium and small European nations can form a sufficiently large economic bloc to be partially independent of the pressure exerted by globalisation to adopt the 'American model' of market-determination and flexible labour markets, in favour of a 'European model' characterised by a social market approach. The creation of a European Social Model, discussed in greater detail in Chapters 2 and 8, is one example of this argument.

By contrast, opponents of EU membership argue that the restrictions placed upon UK sovereignty, imposed by EU membership, are of a different scope and nature from the obligations involved in membership of other international organisations (i.e. UN, GATT/WTO, NATO, EFTA) because none of these can make laws which automatically take precedence over UK legislation. In terms of economic policy, the Treaty of Rome removes the retained power, held by the British government, to prevent the take-over of a UK company by foreign capital, whilst statutory bodies are prohibited from discriminating against contractors from other member states, thereby ending the system of crown preference, and enforcing compulsory competitive tendering, across the union. Types of industrial policy are also outlawed, including initiatives intended to provide short-term protection against aggressive take-over by competitors for a fledgling company with excellent competitive future prospects, or subsidising export-led growth development. The UK is prevented from regulating inward and outward flows of capital, thereby weakening democratic control over the economy, and raising the probability of the economy being rocked by speculative short term flows having little or no relation to the underlying economic fundamentals of the economy. Immigration and manpower policy will be affected by the EU rule in favour of unlimited movement of labour across member states. Moreover, the desire to create a common internal market across all EU member states prevents national governments from raising impediments to this free trade, whether intended to protect workers, consumers and/or the environment.

Orthodox political economists would claim that these interventionist policies are not only 'out of date' in contemporary circumstances, but that they represent sub-optimal economic policy options. Nevertheless, the fact remains that EU membership does indeed constrain national governments from pursuing certain types of economic and political policies, and therefore limits national sovereignty. The question rather shifts to whether governments would actually *want* to pursue such policy options rather than less interventionist, neo-liberal alternatives.

A second example that could be included in this discussion, relates to the appropriate level of government for fiscal policy determination within the EU. Within federal systems, fiscal policy assignment typically results in a division between central and decentralised functions, with the former assuming responsibility for macroeconomic stabilisation and a degree of income redistribution between localities or regions, whereas decentralised government provides goods and services whose consumption is limited to their own jurisdiction, and raises localised income accordingly (Oates, 2004). In the case of the EU, therefore, there are pressures to enhance the central, or federal (European), level of fiscal competence, through transfer of further fiscal authority from national level. However, this is resisted by those national governments that wish to maintain this element of national economic independence, through the unhindered determination of economic strategy. Moreover, emphasis upon retention of sovereignty over tax policy is more significant to Britain than simply the retention of a vital economic lever, but, moreover, because it was in parliamentary assertion of its rights over taxation that the shift from autocracy towards democracy became manifest. Thus, for the British, the issue is as much a question of self-definition as economics (Johnson, 2002:196).

Reasserting national sovereignty

One early critic of UK membership of the EU, namely Aneurin Bevan, accepted the fact that this argument was superficially persuasive, but that the preservation of national sovereignty was the best means for governments to pursue their objectives. He argued that:

> ... the nation is too small an area in which to hope to bring the struggle [for democratic socialism] to a final conclusion. It is true whether the nation is large or small. Thus the attainment of political power in the modern state still leaves many problems outside its scope. National Sovereignty is a phrase that history is emptying of meaning...Many seeing this are inclined to turn away from the difficult task of establishing Socialism in their own country. They say, 'What is the use of doing so? We shall find ourselves possessed of only a partial victory. Only world victory will suffice, so let us concentrate on that.' This is an engaging view and many have succumbed to it. If you are going to plan the world you must first of all control the part of it that you want to fit into the whole. (Bevan, 1952:170–01)

Essentially, Bevan's argument was that, if a party of government wants to create a type of politics internationally, which for Bevan meant progressive, then you need to first implement that vision at home, amidst a national territory where they had greater control of policy levers, and a greater degree of moral legitimacy to implement changes sanctioned through democratic mandate.

As a first step, it has been suggested that this position should be clarified through the passing of a new Act of Parliament, restating the supremacy of parliamentary law over the pronouncements of the ECJ, secured through the modification of the 1972 European Communities Act (Redwood, 2001:164). Although this would seek to clarify the ultimate source of legal sovereignty and would appear to be a necessary step to reasserting national sovereignty, it is not by itself sufficient, as it does not deal with the *use* of sovereign power.

There have been a number of initiatives that have advocated an alternative form of inter-governmental co-operation between European nations, which would acknowledge and support national sovereign independence, whilst recognising the importance of joint endeavour to tackle specific issues of joint importance. Issues could include environmental sustainability and the development of a new system of financial regulation, perhaps similar in scope, if not necessarily in design, to the Bretton Woods arrangement. For example, Tony Benn presented a Commonwealth of Europe Bill in the House of Commons in June 1992, seeking to redesign an intergovernmental forum to facilitate co-operation whilst respecting the democratic traditions of independent member states (Benn and Hood, 1993:114–17; Benn, 2007). Similarly, the Green Party in terms of the 'Europe of the regions' model emphasised decentralised groupings of nations and regions, embracing local self-reliance and resource conservation, with power resting locally and nationally rather than relying upon subsidiarity to filter a fraction of authority of the power accumulated at the centre (Bomberg, 1998).

In contrast, Conservative Party attachment to the nation state and national identity gives Conservative euroscepticism much of its distinctiveness and potency, resulting in a number of identifiable characteristics. These primarily relate to sovereignty, whereby the ultimate decision-making authority of parliament has been eroded by EU membership, together with sovereignty being equated with autonomy, such that Conservative governments of the 1990s lacked autonomy, as they were unable to either decisively shape or block further integration. Additionally, this notion is extended to view European integration possessing an adverse impact on parliamentary sovereignty and the Union, which are regarded as guiding principles of the British constitution. Hence, sovereignty is linked with self-government and nationhood, with the nation state is the legitimate location of sovereign authority. Thus future economic developments such as EMU membership would erode monetary sovereignty. Consequently, following the 1997 general election, the Conservatives sought to restore the primacy of the sovereign nation state through a series of policies on flexibility, renegotiation, reserve powers and the fundamental reform of the EU that envisaged a different relationship between the UK and the EU (Crowson, 2007).

The essential element in all of these, rather diverse, alternatives is to redesign EU institutions and collaborative arrangements which accept the reality of national sovereignty and seek to identify areas where independent nation states will wish to co-operate to their mutual advantage. This is quite different from the present approach, which seeks to pursue further and deeper integration, which diminishes the capacity of independent action by member states. It is not, however, as certain commentators argue, an argument for a 'two-speed Europe', because this suggests that all participants are travelling in the same direction, only some are faster to reach the destination than others (Redwood, 2001:174).

Notes

[1] For more detailed discussion on the 1975 UK Referendum on continued membership of the Common Market (laterly the EU), see Baimbridge et al (2006) and Baimbridge (2007).

CHAPTER 11

TOWARDS A BRAVE NEW WORLD?

Introduction

This book has debated the nature of Britain's relationship with the European Union. It has sought to answer whether this is largely positive, thereby enabling the exercise of pooled sovereign authority, amidst conditions of globalisation, or alternatively, whether it is unduly restrictive, undermining democratic accountability and self-government with rules and policies which impinge upon those objectives that the nation and its people would actually like to pursue. In essence, we ask whether Britain is *Moored to the Continent* as a reluctant partner, too timid or unimaginative to pursue an alternative form of inter-governmental co-operation with its regional neighbours, or is it a misunderstood, enthusiastic partner in the broader federalist, integrationist project?

This volume has outlined the historical nature of Britain's awkward partnership with the EU. How differences in history, culture and political traditions have made for ill at ease bedfellows. But, moreover, it has demonstrated how EU membership has never really worked for the UK, with persistent trade deficits and the smaller than anticipated gains accruing from the creation of a single European market, such that EU membership failed to make economic sense even in the narrow area of trade agreements. Moreover, high agricultural subsidies, the devastation of British fisheries, high net budgetary contributions and unwanted regulatory interferences in British life, made EU membership unpopular, even without the single currency, proposed European constitutions and moves towards closer political integration. This is not simply a case of regulation and harmonisation, but rather scepticism goes to the very essence of what EU membership was supposed to achieve whereby the economic cost-benefit estimate looks decidedly unattractive.

This is particularly disappointing for supporters of the integration process, but it need not be fatal to their basic approach if it were proven that, even if membership has been rather costly to date, there is, nevertheless, no real alternative to its maintenance. Thus, arguments are presented that emphasise the powerful forces unleashed by globalisation, which hollow out the nation state, necessitating the development of super-national forms of governmental authority to prevent market forces from making national regulation and economic policy instruments irrelevant. This is a particularly relevant argument to progressive political parties, since they wish to use the tools available to the state to moderate market distribution and to more closely manage economic developments. Thus, pooling sovereignty, through the EU or other international organisations, would empower the European citizenry.

Once again, however, the evidence presented in this book contradicts this point of view. For example, the economic framework, established by the EU, is decidedly deflationary in nature, deliberately constraining the autonomy of national governments in terms of monetary and (counter-cyclical) fiscal policy. Moreover, as the events of 2010 and 2011 have illustrated in relation to Greece, Ireland and Portugal, EMU is unlikely to work to the benefit of all of its diverse participants, given persistent differences in industrial structures, financial and labour markets. The present structure, without compensatory fiscal federalism, is likely to remain plagued by asymmetric shocks, whereby the turnaround in Ireland's fortunes is only one obvious example. The political structure, likewise, detracts from national priorities. It is inadequately democratic, with weak accountability and transparency, whilst the derogation of powers to Brussels weakens the national democratic process. Consequently, membership narrows the range of options that mainstream political parties can present to the electorate, resulting in disaffection from the political process and an electoral opportunity for more extremist perspectives as witnessed with the election of two BNP candidates to the European Parliament in June 2009.

Moreover, there are always alternatives to any policy option. Each will, of course, have its own consequences, and it is for governments and voters to determine whether a potential benefit is worth the associated cost involved in its pursuit. Thus, the third section of the book outlined a number of the myriad of alternative options available to the British government. In the area of trade, these may involve a measure of renegotiation of trade agreements, consideration of alternative trade institutions (i.e. EFTA II, NAFTA), or embracing greater degrees of independence, perhaps of a similar nature to that adopted by Norway, Switzerland or Greenland. In social and employment policy, the choice should not be between a European Social Model and a brutal form of market-based determination, but rather consideration of whether 'flexicurity' and active employment measures could be better combined within or without the constraints imposed by the single market and EU social regulation. Thus, the real question is whether it is possible for nation states to create something that the EU has conspicuously failed to achieve, namely to protect and enable workers and citizens without having unduly costly regulatory side-effects upon small businesses? Finally, governments might wish to consider whether the repatriation of powers to national parliaments might facilitate greater democratic participation, since voting can affect more aspects of individual lives. Naturally, some of these decisions might lead to policies with which specific individuals might not like, but this is the essence of democracy, and not an argument to maintain EU arrangements to frustrate unwelcome expressions of democratic opinion.

However, a greater repatriation of authority to national governments, whether in full or in part, is only the first step. This, in and of itself, provides the means by which a new national strategy can be enacted, and new collaborative international arrangements can be forged. It may lead to a market-orientated, market-liberal, conservative approach, emphasising competition, flexibility and conforming to market determined norms. Alternatively, it might enable the development of a progressive, Keynesian consensus, promoting full employment, industrial regeneration and progressive redistribution. Or, again, it may deliver an approach focusing upon an environmental sustainability, with all of the implications for energy, housing and transportation sectors that this implies. Each of these visions is markedly different in terms of what it is trying to achieve, and which policy instruments it proposes using, and yet each shares the key element that it is up to the British people to determine their own fate. And, perhaps, one might suggest, that is the way it should be!

BIBLIOGRAPHY

Abbott, D. (2000). 'The case against the Maastricht model of central bank independence'; in Baimbridge, M., Burkitt, B. and Whyman, P. (eds) *The Impact of the Euro: Debating Britain's Future*, Macmillan, London.

Ackrill, R. (2005). 'The Common Agricultural Policy'; in van der Hoek, M.P. (ed.) *Handbook of Public Administration and Policy in the European Union*, CRC Press, New York.

Albert, M. (1993). *Capitalism Against Capitalism*, Whurr, London.

Amoroso, B. and Jespersen, J. (1992). Macroeconomic Theories and Policies for the 1990s: A Scandinavian Perspective, St Martins Press, New York.

Aspinwall, M. (2003). 'Britain and Europe: some alternative economic tests', *Political Quarterly*, 74 (2), 146–57.

Baimbridge, M. (2006). 'The ECB in theory and practice'; in Whyman, P., Baimbridge, M. and Burkitt, B. (eds) *Implications of the Euro: A Critical Perspective from the Left*, Routledge, London

Baimbridge, M. (ed.) (2007). The 1975 Referendum on Europe: Reflections of the Participants, Imprint Academic, Exeter.

Baimbridge, M. and Whyman, P. (2004). *Fiscal Federalism and European Economic Integration*, Routledge, London.

Baimbridge, M. and Whyman, P. (2008). *Britain, the Euro and Beyond*, Ashgate: Aldershot.

Baimbridge, M., Burkitt, B. and Macey, M. (1994). 'The Maastricht Treaty: exacerbating racism in Europe?', *Ethnic and Racial Studies*, 17 (3), 420–41.

Baimbridge, M., Burkitt, B. and Whyman, P. (1998). *Is Europe Ready for EMU? Theory, Evidence and Consequences*, Occasional Paper 31, The Bruges Group, London.

Baimbridge, M., Burkitt, B. and Whyman, P. (1999). 'Economic convergence and EMU membership: theory and evidence', *Journal of European Integration*, 21 (4) 281–305.

Baimbridge, M., Burkitt, B. and Whyman, P. (1999). *The Bank that Rules Europe? The ECB and Central Bank Independence*, Occasional Paper 37, The Bruges Group, London.

Baimbridge, M., Burkitt, B. and Whyman, P. (2000). 'An overview of European monetary integration'; in Baimbridge, M., Burkitt, B. and Whyman, P. (eds) *The Impact of the Euro: Debating Britain's Future*, Macmillan, London.

Baimbridge, M., Burkitt, B. and Whyman, P. (2005). *Britain and the European Union: Alternative Futures*, CIB, London.

Baimbridge, M., Harrop, J. and Philippidis, G. (2004). *Current Economic Issues in EU Integration*, Palgrave Macmillan, London.

Baimbridge, M., Whyman, P. and Mullen, A. (2007). *The 1975 Referendum on Europe: Current Analysis and Lessons for the Future*, Imprint Academic, Exeter.

Baker, D., Gamble, A. and Seawright, D. (2002). 'Sovereign nations and global markets: modern British Conservatism and hyperglobalism', *British Journal of Politics and International Relations*, 4 (3), 399–428.

Balanya, B., Doherty, A., Hoedeman, O., Ma'anit, A. and Wesselius, E. (2000). *Europe Inc.*, Pluto Press, London.

Barclay, R. (1960). Memorandum, 26 June, London, Public Records Office, FO 371/150360

Barnard, C. and Deakin, S. (1997). 'European Community social law and policy: evolution or regression?', *Industrial Relations Journal* (European Annual Review) 131–53.

Barnett, R.J. and Cavanagh, J. (1994). *Global Dreams: Imperial Corporations and the New World Order*, Simon and Schuster, New York.

Barr, N. (1992). 'Economic theory and the Welfare State: a survey and interpretation', *Journal of Economic Literature*, 30, 741–803.

Bayoumi, T. and Eichengreen, B. (1993). 'Shocking aspects of European monetary integration'; in Torres, F. and Giavazzi, F. (eds) *Adjustment and Growth in the European Monetary Union*, Cambridge University Press, Cambridge.

Bean, C., Bentolila, S., Bertola, G. and Dolado, J. (1998). *Social Europe: One for All?*, Centre for Economic Policy Research, London.

Benn, T. (2006). 'The establishment of a Commonwealth of Europe'; in Whyman, P., Baimbridge, M. and Burkitt, B. (eds) *Implications of the Euro: A Critical Perspective from the Left*, Routledge, London.

Benn, T. (2007). 'The establishment of a Commonwealth of Europe', in Whyman, P., Baimbridge, M. and Burkitt, B. (eds) *Implications of the Euro: A Critical Perspective from the Left*, Routledge, London, pp. 186–95.

Benn, T. and Hood, A. (1993). *Common Sense: A New Constitution for Britain*, Hutchinson, London.

Bevan, A. (1952). *In Place of Fear*, Heinnemann, London.

Black, C.M. (2000). The European Union, Britain and the United States: Which Way To Go?, Nixon Center Perspectives, 4 (2).

Blair, A. (2000). *Managing Change: A National and International Agenda of Reform?*, speech given at the World Economic Forum, Davos, Switzerland, 28 January.

Bomberg, E. (1998). Green Parties and Politics in the European Union, Routledge, London.

Bordo, M. and Jonung, L. (2000). *Lessons for EMU from the History of Monetary Unions*, IEA Readings 50, Institute of Economic Affairs, London.

Boyer , R. and Drache, D. (1996) (eds). *States Against Markets*, Routledge, London.

Broad, R. (2001). Labour's European Dilemmas: From Bevin to Blair, Palgrave, Basingstoke.

Broad, R. and Geiger, T. (1996). 'The 1975 referendum on Europe: a witness seminar', *Contemporary Record*, 10 (3), 82–105.

Brown, G. (2010). Beyond the Crash: Overcoming the First Crisis of Globalisation, Simon and Schuster, London.

Bruno, M. and Sachs, J. (1985). *Economics of World-wide Stagflation*, Harvard University Press, Boston.

Buechtemann, C.F. and Schupp, J. (1992). 'Repercussions of reunification: patterns and trends in the socio-economic transformation of East Germany', *Industrial Relations Journal*, 23 (2), 90–106.

Bulmer, S. and Burch, M. (1998). 'Organising for Europe: Whitehall, the British state and the European Union', *Public Administration*, 76, 601–28.

Burkitt, B. (1975) Britain and the European Economic Community: A Political Re-appraisal, British Business for World Markets, Shipley.

Burkitt, B. and Baimbridge, M. (1990). 'The performance of British agriculture and the impact of the Common Agricultural Policy: a historical review', *Rural History*, 1 (2), 265–80.

Burkitt, B. and Baimbridge, M. (1990). 'Britain, the European Economic Community and the single market of 1992: a reappraisal', *Journal of Public Money and Management*, 10 (4), 57–61.

Burkitt, B. and Baimbridge, M. (1991). 'The Cecchini Report and the impact of 1992', *European Research*, 2 (5), 16–19.

Burkitt, B., Baimbridge, M. and Reed, S. (1992). From Rome to Maastricht: A Reappraisal of Britain's Membership of the European Community, Anglia Press, Sudbury.

Burkitt, B., Baimbridge, M. and Whyman, P. (1996). *There is an Alternative: Britain and its Relationship with the EU*, Nelson and Pollard, Oxford.

Butler, D. and Kitzinger, U. (1976). *The 1975 Referendum*, Macmillan, London.

Cabinet Office (1961). Minutes of Cabinet Meeting, 20 April, London, Public Records Office CAB 134/1821.

Callaghan, J. (2000). *The Retreat of Social Democracy*, Manchester University Press, Manchester.

Calmfors, L. and Driffill, J. (1988). 'Bargaining structure, corporatism and macroeconomic performance', *Economic Policy*, 6, 13–62.

Carnoy, M., Cohen, S. and Cardoso, F.H (1993). *The New Global Economy in the Information Age,* Pennsylvania State University Press, University Park, PA.

Castells, M. (1996). The Information Age: Economy, Society and Culture, Blackwell, Oxford.

Castells, M. (2000). 'Information technology and global capitalism'; in Hutton, W. and Giddens, A. (eds) *On the Edge: Living with Global Capitalism*, Jonathan Cape, London, pp. 52–75.

Cecchini, P. (1988). The European Challenge—The Benefits of a Single Market, Wildwood House, Aldershot.

Cerny, P.G. (1990). The Changing Architecture of Politics: Structure, Agency and the Future of the State, Sage, London.

Cerny, P.G. (1997). 'The deregulation and re-regulation of financial markets in a more open world'; in Cerny, P.G. (ed.) *Finance and World Politics Markets, Regimes and States in the Post-hegemonic Era,* Edward Elgar, Aldershot.

Church, C. (1993). 'Switzerland and Europe: problem or pattern?' *European Policy Forum.*

Clark, I. (1997). Globalization and Fragmentation: International Relations in the Twentieth Century, Oxford University Press, Oxford.

Coates, D. (1999). 'Models of capitalism in the new world order', *Political Studies*, 47, 643–60.

Crafts, N. (2000). 'Globalization and growth in the twentieth century', *International Monetary Fund Working Paper*, IMF, Washington DC.

Crowson, N.J. (2007). The Conservative Party and European Integration since 1945: At the Heart of Europe?, Routledge, London.

Daniels, P. (2003). 'From hostility to 'constructive engagement': the Europeanisation of the Labour Party'; in Chadwick, A. and Heffernan, R. (eds) *The New Labour Reader*, Polity Press, Cambridge, pp. 223–30.

Deva, N. (2002). *Who Really Governs Britain?*, The June Press, Totnes.

Dicken, P. (1992). *Global Shift,* Paul Chapman Publishing, London.

Dunning, J.H. (1988). *Multinationals, Technology and Competitiveness*, Unwin Hyman, Boston, MA.

Eatwell, J. (1995). 'The international origins of unemployment'; in Michie, J. and Grieve Smith, J. (eds) *Managing the Global Economy*, Oxford University Press, Oxford.

Eatwell, J. (2000). 'Unemployment: national policies in a global economy', *International Journal of Manpower*, 21 (5), 343–73.

Eichengreen, B. (1990). 'One money for Europe? Lessons from the US currency union', *Economic Policy*, 10, 117–88.

Eichengreen, B. (2010). 'Out-of-the-box thoughts about the international financial architecture', *Journal of International Commerce, Economics and Policy*, 1 (1), 1–20.

Esping-Andersen, G. (1990). *The Three Worlds of Welfare Capitalism*, Polity Press, Cambridge.

EU (2000). 'European social agenda', in Presidency Conclusions: Nice European Council Meeting, 7–9 December, EN SN 400/00, ADD1 (Annex 1).

EU Commission (1992). *Treaty on European Union*, Office for the Official Publications of the European Communities, Luxembourg.

EU Commission (2006). 'Enlargement, two years after: an economic evaluation', *European Economy*, Occasional Paper 24, EU Commission, Brussels.

Eurostat Yearbook (1998–99). *A Statistical Eye on Europe Data 1987–1997*, Office for Official Publications of the European Communities, Luxembourg.

Eurostat Yearbook (2005). *Europe in Figures:*, Office for Official Publications of the European Communities, Luxembourg.

Favretto, I. (2003). The Long Search for a Third Way: The British Labour Party and the Italian Left since 1945, Palgrave, MacMillan.

Feld, L.P. (2005). 'European public finances: much ado about nothing'; in van der Hoek, M.P. (ed.) *Handbook of Public Administration and Policy in the European Union*, CRC Press, New York.

Feldstein, M.S. (1974). 'Social security, induced retirement and aggregate capital accumulation', *Journal of Political Economy*, 82, 905–26.

Feldstein, M.S. (1976). 'Temporary layoffs in the theory of unemployment', *Journal of Political Economy*, 84, 937–57.

Flockton, C. (1998). 'Germany's long-running fiscal strains: unification costs or unsustainability of welfare state arrangements?', *Debatte: Journal of Contemporary Central and Eastern Europe*, 6 (1), 9–93.

Garrett, G. (1995). 'Capital mobility, trade and the domestic politics of economic policy', *International Organisation*, 49, 657–87.

George, S. (ed.) (1992). Britain and the European Community: The Politics of Semi-detachment, Clarendon Press, Oxford.

George, S. (1998). *An Awkward Partner: Britain in the European Community*, Oxford University Press, Oxford.

Giddens, A. (2002). *Where Now for New Labour?*, Fabian Society, London.

Giddens, A. and Hutton, W. (2000). 'In conversation', in Hutton, W. and Giddens, A. (eds) *On the Edge: Living with Global Capitalism*, Jonathan Cape, London, pp. 1–52.

Gill, S. (1998) 'Economic governance and the new constitutionalism', *New Political Economy*, 3 (1), pp. 5–26.

Glyn, A and Sutcliffe, B. (1992). 'Global but leaderless: the new capitalist order', Miliband, R. (ed.) *The Socialist Register*, Sage, London, pp. 76–95.

Goodhart, C.A.E. (1995). 'The political economy of monetary union'; in Kenen, P.B. (ed.) *Understanding Independence: The Macroeconomics of the Open Economy*, Princeton University Press, Princeton.

Gould, B. (2006). 'Preface'; in Whyman, P., Baimbridge, M. and Burkitt, B. (eds) *Implications of the Euro: A Critical Perspective from the Left*, Routledge, London.

Grant, W. (2002). *Economic Policy in Britain*, Palgrave, London.

Harrison, B. (1996). *The Transformation of British Politics 1860–1995*, Oxford University Press, Oxford.

Harrop, J. (2005). 'The internal market'; in van der Hoek, M.P. (ed.) *Handbook of Public Administration and Policy in the European Union*, CRC Press, New York.

Harvey, D. (1995). The Return of the Strong: The Drift to Global Disorder, Macmillan, London.

Hay, C. (1999). The Political Economy of New Labour: Labouring Under False Pretences?, Manchester University Press, Manchester.

Heath, E. (2000). 'Sovereignty in the modern world'; in Baimbridge, M., Burkitt, B. and Whyman, P. (eds) *The Impact of the Euro: Debating Britain's Future*, Macmillan, Basingstoke, pp. 203–09.

Helleiner, E. (2000). 'Explaining the globalization of financial markets: bringing states back in'; in Higgott, R. and Payne, A. (eds) *The New Political Economy of Globalisation, Volume One*, Edward Elgar, Cheltenham.

Hettne, B. (1994). 'The regional factor in the formation of a new world order'; in Sakamoto, Y. (eds) *Global Transformation: Challenges to the State System*, United Nations University, Tokyo, pp. 134–66.

Heywood, A. (1999). *Key Concepts in Politics*, Macmillan, Basingstoke.

Higgott, R. and Payne, A. (2000). 'Introduction: towards a new political economy of globalisation'; in Higgott, R. and Payne, A. (eds) *The New Political Economy of Globalisation, Volume One*, Edward Elgar, Cheltenham.

Hindley, B. and Howe, M. (1996). *Better-off out? The Benefits or Costs of EU Membership*, IEA Occasional Paper 99, Institute of Economic Affairs, London.

Hirst, P. and Thompson, G. (1996). Globalisation in Question: The International Economy and the Possibilities of Governance, Polity, Cambridge.

HM Treasury (1997). 'UK Membership of the Single Currency: an assessment of the Five Economic Tests', HM Treasury, London.

HMG (1971). The United Kingdom and the European Communities, Cmnd.4715, London: HMSO.

Hofstede, G. (1980). *Culture's Consequences*, Sage, London.

Holland, S. (1995). 'Squaring the circle? The Maastricht Convergence criteria, cohesion and employment', in Coates, K. and Holland, S. (eds) *Full Employment for Europe*, Spokesman, Nottingham.

Holstein, W.J. (1990). 'The stateless corporation', *Business Week*, 14 May, pp. 52–9.

Horn, G.A. and Zwiener, R. (1992). 'Wage regimes in a united Europe'; in Barrell, R. and Whitley, J. (eds) *Macroeconomic Policy Co-ordination in Europe*, Sage, London, pp. 83–101.

Jackman, R., Pissarides, C. and Savouri, S. (1990). 'Labour market policies and unemployment in the OECD', *Economic Policy*, 5 (2), 449–90.

Jamieson, B. (1998). *Britain: Free to Choose*, Global Britain, London.

Jarvis, V. and Prais, S.J. (1989). 'Two nations of shopkeepers', *National Institute Economic Review*, 128, May, 58–74.

Jay, D. (1990). *The European Monetary System: The ERM Illusion*, Labour Common Market Safeguards Committee, London.

Jessop, B. (1993). 'Towards a Schumpeterian Workfare State? Preliminary remarks on post-Fordist political economy studies', *Political Economy*, 40.

Jessop, B. (1994). 'Post-Fordism and the state', in Amin, A. (ed.) *Post Fordism: A Reader*, Blackwell, Oxford.

Johnson, N. (2002). 'Can self-government survive? Britain and the European Union'; in Holmes, M. (ed.) *The Eurosceptical Reader 2*, Palgrave, Basingstoke, pp. 184–225.

Kapstein, E.B. (1994). *Governing the Global Economy: International Finance and the State*, Harvard University Press, Cambridge, MA.

Katz, P.L. (1988). The Information Society: An International Perspective, Praeger, New York.

Keller, B. and Sorries, B. (1997). 'The new social dialogue: procedural structuring, first results and perspectives', *Industrial Relations Journal* (European Annual Review), 77–98.

Kenen, P.B. (1969). 'The theory of optimum currency areas: an eclectic view'; in Mundell, R.A. and Swoboda, A.K. (eds) *Monetary Problems of the International Economy*, University of Chicago Press, Chicago.

Keynes, J.M. (1920). *The Economic Consequences of the Peace*, Penguin, London, 1988 edition.

Keynes, J.M. (1942). *Collected Works*, 25, pp. 108–39, Macmillan, London.

Kopits, G. (1992) (ed.). Tax Harmonisation in the European Community: Policy Issues and Analysis, IMF, Washington DC.

Korpi, W. (1996). 'Eurosclerosis and the sclerosis of objectivity: on the role of values among economic policy experts', *Economic Journal*, 106 (439), 1727–46.

Korten, D. (1995). *When Corporations Rule the World*, Kumarian Press, West Hartford, Conneticut.

Kydland, F.E. and Prescott, E.C. (1977). 'Rules rather than discretion: the time inconsistency of optimal plans', *Journal of Political Economy*, 85, 473–99.

Labour Party (1962). *Annual Conference Report*, Labour Party, London.

Lang, T. and Hines, C. (1993). The New Protectionism: Protecting the Future Against Free Trade, Earthscan, London.

Lawrence, R. and Schultz, C. (1987) (eds). *Barriers to European Growth: A Transatlantic View*, Brokings Institution, Washington DC.

Leach, G. (2000). 'EU membership: what's the bottom line?' IoD Policy Paper, Institute of Directors, London.

Leibfried, S, (1994). 'The social dimension of the European Union: en route to positively joint sovereignty?', *Journal of European Social Policy*, 4 (4), 239–62.

Leibfried, S. and Pierson, P. (1995). 'The dynamics of social policy integration'; in Leibfried, S. and Pierson, P. (eds) *Fragmented Social Policy: the European Community's Social Dimension in Comparative Perspective*, Brookings Institution, Washington DC.

Lindbeck, A., Molander, P., Persson, T., Petersson, O., Sandmo, A., Swedenborg, B. and Thygesen, N. (1994). *Turning Sweden Around*, MIT Press, London.

MacDougall, D. (1992). 'Economic and monetary union and the European Community budget, *National Institute Economic Review*, May, 64–8.

MacDougall, D. (2003). 'Economic and monetary union and the European Community budget'; in Baimbridge, M. and Whyman, P. (eds) *Economic and Monetary Union in Europe: Theory, Evidence and Practice*, Edward Elgar, Cheltenham.

Major, R.L. and Hays, S. (1970). 'Another look at the Common Market, *National Institute Economic Review*, 54, 29–43.

Malcolm, N. (1996). 'Sense on sovereignty'; in Holmes, M. (ed.) *The Eurosceptical Reader*, Macmillan, Basingstoke, pp. 342–67.

Marginson, P. and Sisson, K. (1996). 'Multinational companies and the future of collective bargaining: a review of the research issues', *European Journal of Industrial Relations*, 2 (2), 173–97.

Marquand, D. (1999). 'Premature obsequies: social democracy comes in from the cold'; in Gamble, A. and Wright, T. (eds) *The New Social Democracy*, Blackwell, Oxford.

Marsden, D. (1992). 'Incomes policy for Europe? Or will pay bargaining destroy the Single European Market?', *British Journal of Industrial Relations*, 30 (4), 587–604.

McGrew, A. and Lewis, P. (1992). *Globalisation and the Nation States*, Polity Press, Cambridge.

McKay, D. (1999). Federalism and the European Union: A Political Economy Perspective, Oxford University Press, Oxford.

McKay, D. (2001). Designing Europe: Comparative Lessons from the Federal Experience, Oxford University Press, Oxford.

McKinnon, R. (1963). 'Optimum currency areas', *American Economic Review*, 53, 717–25.

Michie, J. (2000). 'The economic consequences of EMU for Britain'; in Baimbridge, M., Burkitt, B. and Whyman, P. (eds), *The Impact of the Euro: Debating Britain's Future*, Macmillan, London.

Michie, J. (2006). 'Economic consequences of EMU for Britain'; in Whyman, P., Baimbridge, M. and Burkitt, B. (eds) *Implications of the Euro: A Critical Perspective from the Left*, Routledge, London.

Mills, J. (2010). 'Questions and answers on the prospects for the euro', *Labour Euro-Safeguards Campaign Bulletin*, January.

Mills, J. (2011). 'Questions and answers on the future of the euro', *Labour Euro-Safeguards Campaign Bulletin*, January.

Milne, I. (2004). *A Cost Too Far?*, Civitas, London.

Minford, P. (2000). 'The single currency—will it work and should we join?'; in Baimbridge, M., Burkitt, B. and Whyman, P. (eds) *The Impact of the Euro: Debating Britain's Future*, Macmillan. London.

Minford, P. (2002). *Should Britain Join The Euro*?, Institute of Economic Affairs, London.

Minford, P., Mahambare, V. and Nowell, E. (2005). *Should Britain Leave the EU? An Economic Analysis of a Troubled Relationship*, Edward Elgar, Cheltenham.

Minsky, H. (2008). *John Maynard Keynes*, McGraw-Hill, London.

Mitchell, A. (2006). 'Euro versus the people'; in Whyman, P., Baimbridge, M. and Burkitt, B. (eds) *Implications of the Euro: A Critical Perspective from the Left*, Routledge, London.

Mullen, A. (2010). 'Economic and political sovereignty: the progressive case'; in Baimbridge, M., Whyman, P. and Burkitt, B. (eds) *Britain in a Global World: Options for a New Beginning*, Imprint Academic, Exeter.

Mullen, A. and Burkitt, B. (2004). Spinning Europe: Pro-European Union Propaganda Campaigns in Britain, Democrat Press, Merseyside.

Mundell, R.A. (1961). 'A theory of optimum currency areas', *American Economic Review*, 51, 657–65.

Naisbitt, J. (1994). Global Paradox: The Bigger the World Economy, the More Powerful its Smallest Players, Brealey, London.

O'Connor, M. (2009). 'The euro meltdown', *European Journal*, December, p. 3.

Oates, W.E. (2004). 'An essay on fiscal federalism'; in Baimbridge, M. and Whyman, P.B. (eds) *Fiscal Federalism and European Economic Integration*, Routledge, London, pp. 13–47.

Obstfeld, M. and Taylor, A. (1997). 'The Great Depression as a watershed: international capital mobility over the long run', CEPR *Discussion Paper Series*, no. 1633.

OECD (1996). Trade, Employment and Labour Standards: A Study of Core Workers' Rights and International Trade, OECD, Paris.

Ohmae, K. (1990). The Borderless World: Power and Strategy in the Interlinked Economy, Collins, London.

Ohmae, K. (1993). 'The rise of the region state', *Foreign Affairs*, 71 (2), 78–87.

Ohmae, K. (1995). The End of the Nation-State: The Rise of Regional Economies, Harper Collins, London.

Ormerod, P. (1999). 'The Euro-attack on jobs'; in Bush, J. (ed.), *Everything You Always Wanted to Know About the Euro*, New Europe, London.

Ormerod, P. (2006). 'The euro: an outsider's perspective'; in Whyman, P., Baimbridge, M. and Burkitt, B. (eds) *Implications of the Euro: A Critical Perspective from the Left*, Routledge, London.

Owen, D. (2006). 'Foreword'; in Whyman, P., Baimbridge, M. and Burkitt, B. (eds) *Implications of the Euro: A Critical Perspective from the Left*, Routledge, London.

Pain, N. and Young, G. (2004). 'The macroeconomic impact of UK withdrawal from the EU', *Economic Modelling*, 21 (3), 387–408.

Palley, T.I. (1999). 'International finance and global deflation: there is an alternative'; in Michie, J. and Grieve Smith, J. (eds) *Global Instability: The Political Economy of World Economic Governance*, Routledge, London.

Panitch, L. (1994). 'Corporatism in liberal democracies'; in Lehmbruch, G. and Schmitter, P (eds) *Socialist Register 1994*, Sage, London.

Patel, P. and Pavitt, K. (1991). 'Large firms in the production of the world's technology: an important case of non-globalisation', *Journal of International Business Studies*, 22 (1), 1–21.

Peele, G. (2004). Governing the UK: British Politics in the 21st Century, Blackwell, Oxford.

Pennant-Rea, R., Bean, C.R., Begg, D., Hardie, J., Lankester, T., Miles, D.K., Portes, R., Robinson, A. Seabright, P. and Wolf, M. (1997). *The Ostrich and the EMU – Policy Choiçes Facing the UK*, Centre for Economic Policy Research, London.

Perraton, J., Goldblatt, D., Held, D. and McGrew, A. (2000). 'The globalisation of economic activity'; in Higgott, R. and Payne, A. (eds) *The New Political Economy of Globalisation, Volume One*, Edward Elgar, Cheltenham.

Petrella, R. (1996). 'Globalization and internationalization: the dynamics of the emerging world order'; in Boyer, R. and Drache, D. (eds) *States Against Markets: The Limits of Globalization*, Routledge, London, pp. 62–83.

Philippidis, G. (2004). 'Membership of NAFTA: a viable alternative for UK agro-food producers?', *Economic Issues*, 9 (2), 21–42.

Pissarides, C. (1997). 'The need for labour market flexibility in European economic and monetary union', *Swedish Economic Policy Review*, 4 (2), 513–46.

Porter, M.E. (1990). *The Competitive Advantage of Nations*, Macmillan, London.

Prais, S.J. and Wagner, K. (1988). 'Productivity and management: the training in foremen in Britain and Germany', *National Institute Economic Review*, 123, February, 34–47.

Redwood, J. (1997). Our Currency, Our Country: The Dangers of European Monetary Union, Penguin Books, London.

Redwood, J. (2000). 'Sterling democracy or European bureaucracy?'; in Baimbridge, M., Burkitt, B. and Whyman, P. (eds) *The Impact of the Euro: Debating Britain's Future*, Macmillan, London.

Redwood, J. (2001). Stars and Strife: The Coming Conflicts between the USA and the European Union, Palgrave, Basingstoke.

Reich, R. (1992). *The Work of Nations*, Vintage, New York.

Rhodes, M. (1992). 'The future of the social dimension': labour market regulation in post-1992 Europe', *Journal of Common Market Studies*, 30 (1), 23-51.

Richards, D. and Smith, M.J. (2002). *Governance and Public Policy in the United Kingdom*, Oxford University Press, Oxford.

Rodrik, D. (1996). *Has Globalization Gone Too Far?* Institute for Research Economics, Washington, DC.

Royal Society of Edinburgh (2004). Inquiry into the Future of the Scottish Fishing Industry, RSE, Edinburgh.

Ruigrok, W. and van Tulder , R. (1995). *The Logic of International Restructuring*, Routledge, London.

Rustin, M. (2001). 'The third sociological way'; in Arestis, P. and Sawyer, M. (eds) *The Economics of the Third Way: Experiences from Around the World*, Edward Elgar, Cheltenham, pp. 11–25.

Sassoon, D. (1999). 'European social democracy and New Labour: unity in diversity?'; in Gamble, A and Wright, T. (eds) *The New Social Democracy*, Blackwell, Oxford, pp. 19–37.

Sawyer, M. and Arestis, P. (2006). 'What type of European monetary union?'; in Whyman, P., Baimbridge, M. and Burkitt, B. (eds) *Implications of the Euro: A Critical Perspective from the Left*, Routledge, London.

Scholte, J.A. (2000). *Globalisation: A Critical Introduction*, Macmillan, Basingstoke.

Schumpeter, J.A. (1942). *Capitalism, Socialism and Democracy*, George Allen and Unwin, London.

Shore, P. (2006). 'Fighting against federalism'; in Whyman, P., Baimbridge, M. and Burkitt, B. (eds) *Implications of the Euro: A Critical Perspective from the Left*, Routledge, London.

Sisson, K. and Marginson, P. (1995). 'Management: systems, structures and strategy'; in Edwards, P. (ed.) *Industrial Relations: Theory and Practice in Britain*, Blackwell, Oxford, pp. 89–122.

Steedman, H. (1988). 'Vocational training in France and Britain', *National Institute Economic Review*, 126, November, 57–70.

Stewart-Brown, R. (1999a). 'In search of the benefits of the Single Market', *Eurofacts*, 3–4, 23 April.

Stewart-Brown, R. (1999b). 'The economic consequences for the UK of the Single Market', *Eurofacts*, 6–7, 6 August.

Stopford, J. and Strange, S. (1991). *Rival States, Rival Firms: Competition for World Market Shares*, Cambridge University Press, Cambridge.

Strange, G. (1997). 'The British Labour movement and economic and monetary union in Europe', *Capital and Class*, 63, 13–24.

Strange, S. (1994). *States and Markets*, Pinter, London, second edition.

Strange, S. (1996). The Retreat of State: The Diffusion of Power in the World Economy, Cambridge University Press, Cambridge.

Strange, S. (2000). 'The defective state'; in Higgott, R. and Payne, A. (eds) (2000) *The New Political Economy of Globalisation, Volume One*, Edward Elgar, Cheltenham.

Streeck, W. (1992). Social Institutions and Economic Performance: Studies of Industrial Relations in Advanced Capitalist Economies, Sage, London.

Streeck, W. and Schmitter, P.C. (1991). 'From national corporatism to transnational pluralism: organised interests in the Single European Market', *Politics and Society*, vol. 2.

Swank, D. (1998). 'Funding the Welfare State: global taxation of business in advanced market economies', *Political Studies*, 46, 671–92.

Taylor, M. (1995). *A Single Currency – Implications for the UK Economy*, Institute of Directors, London.

Teague, P. (1997). 'Lean production and the German model', *German Politics*, 6 (2), 76–94.

Teague, P. (1998). 'Monetary union and social Europe', *Journal of European Social Policy*, 8 (2), 117–39.

Tindemans, L. (1976). 'European Union (Tindemans Report): Report by Mr. Tindemans to the European Council', *Bulletin of the European Communities*, EC 1/76, EU Commission, Brussels.

Tober D. (1993). 'One world – one vision for business'; in S. Bushrui *et al.* (eds) *Transition to a Global Society*, Oneworld, Oxford, pp. 98–107.

Tobin, J. (1994). 'Speculators tax', *New Economy*, 1, 104–09.

UNCAD [United Nations Conference on Trade and Development] (1993). *World Investment Directory*, vol. 3, United Nations, Geneva.

UNCTAD (1995). *World Investment Report 1995*, United Nations.

UNDP (1999). *Human Development Report 1999*, Oxford University Press, Oxford.

Vandenbroucke, F. (1996). *Globalisation, Inequality and Social Democracy*, Institute for Public Policy Research (IPPR), London.

Vaughan-Whitehead, D.C. (2003). EU Enlargement versus Social Europe? The Uncertain Future of the European Social Model, Edward Elgar: Cheltenham.

Verdun, A. (2005). 'A history of economic and monetary union'; in van der Hoek, M.P. (ed.) *Handbook of Public Administration and Policy in the European Union*, CRC Press, New York.

Wade, R. (1996). 'Globalization and its limits: reports of the death of the national economy are greatly exaggerated'; in Berger, S. and Dore, R. (eds) *National Diversity and Global Capitalism*, Cornell University Press: Ithaca, NY, pp. 60–88.

Walsh, J., Zappala, G. and Brown, W. (1995). 'European integration and the pay policies of British multinational', *Industrial Relations Journal*, 26 (2), pp. 84–96.

Watson, M. (2002). 'Sand in the wheels, or oiling the wheels of international finance? New Labour's appeal to a 'New Bretton Woods'', *British Journal of Politics and International Relations*, 4 (2), 193–221.

Weber, A.A. (1991). 'EMU and asymmetries and adjustment problems in the EMS', in *The Economics of EMU, European Economy*, Special Edition 1.

Weiss, L. (1998). The Myth of the Powerless State: Governing the Economy in a Global Era, Cambridge Polity Press: Cambridge.

West, K. (1995). *Economic Opportunities for Britain and the Commonwealth*, Royal Institute for International Affairs, London.

Whyman, P. (2002). 'British trade unions and EMU', *Industrial Relations*, 41 (3), 467–76.

Whyman, P., Burkitt, B. and Baimbridge, M. (2006). 'A post-Keynesian strategy for the UK economy'; in Whyman, P., Baimbridge, M. and Burkitt, B. (eds) *Implications of the Euro: A Critical Perspective from the Left*, Routledge, London.

Whyman, P.B. (2006). *Third Way Economics*, Palgrave, Basingstoke.

Whyman, P.B. (2007). 'The nature of globalisation and its impact on the UK economy', in House of Commons Treasury Select Committee, *Globalisation: Prospects and Policy Responses*, no. 137, The Stationary Office Ltd, London, EV.165–72.

Windolf, P. (1989). 'Productivity coalitions and the future of European corporatism', *Industrial Relations*, 28 (1), 1–20.

Wiseman, J. (1998). Global Nation: Australia and the Politics of Globalisation, Cambridge University Press, Cambridge.

Wistrich, E. (2001). 'Lessons of the 1975 referendum', in Beetham, R. (ed.) *The Euro Debate: Persuading the People*, Federal Trust, London, pp. 37–47.

Zysman, J. (2000). 'The myth of a "global" economy: enduring national foundations and emerging regional realities'; in Higgott, R. and Payne, A. (eds) *The New Political Economy of Globalisation, Volume One*, Edward Elgar: Cheltenham.

INDEX